THIS

IS MY

BODY

THIS
IS MY
BODY

*Embracing
the Messiness
of Faith and
Motherhood*

Hannah E. Shanks

FRESH AIR BOOKS®

Nashville

For my mother, Deb, who always knew that I could.
For my son, Ezra, who taught me how she knew.

CONTENTS

PROLOGUE

approached the Communion rail with trembling knees. I ripped—"The body of Christ, broken for you"—and dipped—"The blood of Christ, shed for you"—with shaking hands. Earlier in the service, after the special Mother's Day portion of the liturgy, I'd exited the sanctuary to splash cold water on my face and take some deep breaths. The pregnancy test was still on my bathroom counter at home. Three hours before, I'd seen two lines for the first time. Two lines. Two lives. A plus one.

A baby.

I had taken the test because I didn't want to spend Mother's Day in a funk. I wanted to know rather than wonder and later have my hopes dashed. I foolishly had thought that if the test were positive, I would enjoy celebrating the day. And I suppose I would have if I weren't the sort of person who breaks out into hives over major life transitions.

Instead, I spent my first Mother's Day growing increasingly panicked and disconnected from my body. With every word of the liturgy extolling the virtues of mothers, every memory of flowers and brooches handed out on Mother's Days past, the stakes seemed to ratchet ever higher until I found myself repeating my own litany for Mother's Day in my head:

Holy and Merciful God,
I cannot rise to this occasion.
I cannot mimic Mary and say,
"Let it be unto me as you have said."
I'm not big enough to be a mom,
and I don't know how to do this,
so help me, help me, help me.
Thank you. Thank you. Thank you.
Amen. Amen. Amen.

When the church began its Communion ritual, I heard the liturgy as though for the first time: "This is my body." The words echoed, and suddenly I came back to myself, came back to my body—my body plus its new, wee traveler. Many years ago, I heard Communion described as the place where we take Christ's body and blood—separated from each other by humanity's lust for control—and put them back together in our own bodies, yielding to the loving will of God. Through this act, I put the body and blood of Christ back together inside my body—and I fed the new life growing inside me. This kneeling-rail experience was the start of a Russian nesting doll of revelations on bodies, faith, Communion, and motherhood that completely reoriented my understanding of the sacramental act of the shared table.

Before I go any further, I want to offer some background information on myself. I'm straight, cisgender, and married. My life happened in such a way that I got pregnant after I got married and not before. I got pregnant on purpose and not by surprise, and I was able to get pregnant with minimal intervention. That's my story, but it's not everyone's story—and I don't expect it to be. I can't tell my story without these parts of myself, but I hope we can stumble across something holy about our shared experiences—even if they're different. Those parts of my story could've happened differently, but what I discovered along the way would still be true: We deserve to inhabit our embodied selves fully, to own every inch of our stories, and to see that some amazing truths and ways of relating to God are open to us if we are willing to see God and God's work in the world through women's experiences in the same way we've seen them through men's experiences for thousands of years.

What follows are stories and insights that have changed my life. These moments of conversion—times when what I saw and touched demanded a change in direction—have shifted my understanding of who God is, who I am, and how we humans can find a way to hang together while other forces work to tear us apart. And we—that is, women and mothers—are not left out of the story. Even when history and church tradition have overlooked our experiences or sanitized them beyond recognition, we've always mattered. Our selves, our bodies, and our experiences have always testified to the glory of God—not only to women who bear children but to everyone.

The words that follow flow from a place of fear converted to freedom. I was nervous and afraid of becoming a mother for all my own reasons and for all the things that twenty-first-century motherhood entails. I also was afraid of becoming a mother in the church, afraid of parenting within the body of Christ. In addition to the millions of unwritten expectations that swirl in the ether outside the church door—expectations about behavior, dress, and parenting choices—the church piles on a million more. The church expects mothers to keep their children "quiet" and "well-behaved" in service, to join the Christian education committee, to work in the nursery, and generally to subsume all their passions, gifts, and projects under the banner of "motherhood." Observing mothers in general, but especially in the church, fueled my anxiety and fear.

Motherhood seemed like a gauntlet set in a minefield. Most of the time, even if women managed to avoid the mines, they still emerged from the field with less of themselves than when they entered. I had watched loved ones take parts of themselves and box them up since they didn't fit under the "mother" label or abandon life-giving activities in their effort to do the "right" thing. And the church—even while joyfully proclaiming freedom and power for all in Christ—often inhabited the front-row seats to the brutal run. I, like so many women of childbearing age, was afraid of being reduced to whatever my womb did or did not yield. My body—whether childless or with child—felt like a blank comments section upon which strangers and church family alike wrote their judgments, speculations, and projections. When I shared my fears with female friends, I quickly found that I wasn't alone. "I think I might want kids one day," one friend confided, "but I don't want to be treated like a mother."

What does it mean to be treated like a mother in church? For me, it meant that I didn't want to be over-sanctified just because I had a child. I didn't want to be forced into nursery duty or into preparing craft projects. I wanted to keep swearing or using whatever language felt appropriate for any given situation and to ignore any traditional boundaries that dictate what mothers are supposed to look, sound, or act like. In short, I wanted children, but I wanted to keep my identity too.

I wanted people in a church family who would walk with me, not covet me for my much desired "young family" demographic. I wanted people who would hold my hands and not let them go when a set of smaller hands appeared on the scene. And for those members of the church who don't want children, I respect their choices and honor them for all the ways they serve the church instead of constantly comparing them to those who are coupled or parenting. Rather than being slotted into a particular marketing demographic or email list based on our status as single, young married, or young family, women want room and space to be themselves without the pressure to couple-up in order to graduate to the married Sunday school class and without fielding questions about whether they plan to reproduce.

This book offers a counter-narrative to the church's reductionist version of motherhood. God is bigger than the boxes we shove God into, and God created us bigger than the boxes we get shoved into. My experience in a woman's body and in a mother's body serves as a conduit and connection to God's life and work in the world, even though many people and institutions believe that a woman has no claim on identifying with God or preaching the gospel. My church attendance has taught me that we talk about God with he/him/his pronouns and not she/her/hers pronouns—words that also describe me. In many churches and denominations, leadership in ministry is completely off the table for women. Though my denomination allows women's ordination, I knew only one female pastor as a child and never saw female clergy represented at ecumenical camps and events. God was for me, but the church as a whole didn't seem to believe I was fit for God. In the end, even though every single one of my fears about motherhood proved true, a larger story emerged. God grew bigger, and so did I. The messages I'd internalized were drowned out by a wave of reckoning.

That wave gained momentum one bright morning at a young clergy conference in Beverly Hills—a place I never expected to visit. As a corn-fed Midwestern girl, I'd always been drawn more to wide-open fields than star-studded streets. On the second morning of the conference, those gathered sang a new song written for worship at that congregation, The Loft LA. The song, titled "She Who Is," fit perfectly at this contemporary Christian church—except for its exclusive use of female attributes, imagery, and pronouns to describe God. Following opening worship, in the fifteen-minute coffee break between sessions, I huddled together with a group of female clergy friends. All around the fellowship hall, similar small huddles of women gathered. All of us appeared to be asking one another the same question: "Have you ever sung a song like that?" And then, with laughter and dawning realization, "Is this how men feel every Sunday?"

In that moment, I felt the power that comes from understanding and identifying with God in words and images that were designed to make God recognizable in the same way that I recognize myself. Finally, I understood that some of the distance I'd felt in church was not simply the distance felt when a mortal tries to reflect on the eternal timelessness of God; it was distance that came from language, translation, and intentional choices that meant God and female were not to occupy the same space, let alone the same sentence. Instead of connecting to God's work *in spite of* my female body, I felt connected to God *because of* my female, birthing, mothering body. When I talked about that connection with others, I watched their understanding of God expand too.

———

I never could comprehend the suffering of the cross. How does a person choose a path that ends in violence and blood? That's how the cross was always presented to me—as a sacrificial death. But what Jesus said of his own work—"This is my body, broken for you; this is my blood, poured out for you"—describes my experience of birth and the experience of every birther who has come before me. And these words, which are used during the liturgy of Communion, also known as Eucharist or the Common Table, create the backbone for this book. Communion is the ritual and act of faith where an assembled body performs what Jesus commands in some of his last words on earth: a shared meal to remember God's offering of God's whole self—body, blood, and life—to bring new, resurrected and abundant life.

We will examine each element of Communion for what it tells us about God, ourselves, one another, and the world, and imagine or re-interpret those elements through a lens of maternity and birth. None of this is meant to exclude people who do not birth or cannot birth but instead to offer a new way of viewing God's work in the world—a way that encourages us to discover how our bodies can help us understand God when we use words and metaphors beyond the typical male-centric language. More than anything, this book is an invitation to try on a different set of lenses, an experiment in freedom, an encouragement to live in truth, and an attempt to close down the motherhood minefield for good.

Ultimately, we can own our bodies and our experiences and the joys and difficulties of motherhood without sugarcoating them. And our boldness in proclaiming what we know—of grief, of sacrifice, of pain, of confusion, of joy, of laughter, of nonsense—are worth more to the church than our silence. Rather than changing our behavior to align with what "Christian motherhood" may include or exclude, we serve both Christianity and motherhood better by pressing against their assumed boundaries.

When we, like Christ, can proclaim, "This is my body," without qualification, caveat, or complaint, we demonstrate what a redemptive life can look like. Whether that body is healthy or ill; upright or stooped; male, female, or gender-queer; light-skinned or dark; scarred, freckled or wrinkled. The truth of our bodies reveals the glory of God. Made perfect in our imperfection, our bodies are enough. Enough to live in and enough to show God's awesomeness. Not *in spite* of our parts or gender but *because* of them.

LITURGY

Irene Zimmerman

All the way to Elizabeth
and in the months afterward
she wove him, pondering,
"This is my body, my blood!"

Beneath the watching eyes
of donkey, ox, and sheep,
she rocked him, crooning,
"This is my body, my blood!"

In the moonless desert flight
and the Egypt days of his growing,
she nourished him, singing,
"This is my body, my blood!"

In the search for her young lost boy
and the foreboding day of his leaving
she let him go, knowing,
"This is my body, my blood!"

Under the blood-smeared cross,
she rocked his mangled bones,

re-membering him, moaning,
"This is my body, my blood!"

When darkness, stones, and tomb
bloomed to Easter morning,
she ran to him, shouting,
"This is my body, my blood!"

And no one thought to tell her:
"Woman, it is not fitting
for you to say those words.
You don't resemble him."

CHAPTER 1

Incarnation

"This is my body that is for you."
—1 Corinthians 11:24

Bodies are important to God.

Our bodies, whatever state they are in right now, are beautiful images of God in the world. God values our bodies—what we do with them and what has been done against them. I believe that we can understand God better when we understand our bodies better, but we must first examine why so many of us—and especially so many women—have a hard time imagining our bodies as anything but a disappointment or afterthought to God.

Wherever and whoever we are, we've inherited scars that we carry, and we need to address them up front. Not because they are obstacles but because they are stories that are too often untold, overlooked, or hidden in shame. And we cannot receive the truth that our bodies are the image of God in the world if we are hiding them from ourselves. We cannot proclaim that God values our bodies when we've been programmed to add too many caveats to that value: God values my body *if* it is covered. *If* it is thin. *If* it is chaste. *If* it is flawless. *If* it is blemish-free. *If* it is pretty. *If* it is healthy. *If* it is young. *If* it is fair-skinned. Understanding that our bodies matter to God is way bigger than how we eat or move or heal or look. Understanding that my body— a woman's body—matters deeply to God and reveals God in the world has flown in the face of what I picked up from church teaching and preaching.

Most of us are taught that our bodies belong to us; our bodies, on their own, are not us but rather "vessels" or "transports," a home for our spirits. This isn't a new idea. This way of thinking is called *dualism*, and it was practiced by ancient Greeks. Our thoughts about spirit being something separate from the body began with them, and their thoughts about denying the body in order to attain higher spiritual insight have stuck around through much of Western thought and Christianity. It also gave rise to the tradition of Gnosticism, which holds the idea that all things of the body are lesser, while things of the spirit are the only true and desirable things worth seeking. Truthfully, most of us probably have some Gnosticism working in our hearts.

The separation of body and spirit is often central to what we learn about our bodies. We are taught to master, escape, tame, train, ignore, use, cover, care for, and guard them. Implicit in this teaching lies the idea that we are doing something *to* our bodies rather than *with* them. We're taught that our bodies are separate from our being but indicators about the goodness of our being. And to this end, we're taught *heresy*—a thorny word, especially for those of us who can hear it in our memories, shouted at us from behind a wagging finger and a scowl of disapproval. But in this instance, we're talking about the literal sense of the word.

Gnosticism and dualism sparked much debate in the second and third centuries CE, and after a few centuries of fighting, the Christian church formally denounced the idea that bodies, flesh, and human experience are dirty, less desirable, or less holy than spiritual matters. In fact, the church went further and stated that body and spirit are not separate but one. Saint Irenaeus argued strenuously against Gnosticism, writing, "For that flesh which has been moulded is not a perfect [human] in itself, but the body of a [human], and part of a [human]. Neither is the soul itself, considered apart by itself, the [human]."[1] In other words, spirit alone isn't enough; flesh is important. But Irenaeus and his issues with Gnosticism were the furthest thing from my mind as a child, trying to navigate becoming an adult and having an adult body. Irenaeus's arguments didn't make it to rural Illinois, but somehow Gnosticism did.

I was raised in a fairly typical Midwestern American church. There I was taught not to find worth in my body. I knew I shouldn't be too proud of it or focus too much on how it looked, since looks are fleeting. I was taught to be kind to others and try to see them the way God sees them, which is how they are on the inside. But this thinking shifted as soon as I hit puberty. Then, the church became very concerned about what I looked like on the outside— and so did the rest of the world.

A man catcalled me for the first time at age eleven as I rode my bike the few blocks to youth group. I was wearing jean shorts and a green dip-dyed T-shirt with silver dragonflies on it. I was all coltish limbs without a whisper of breasts—proof that it's not how one looks or what one wears that's responsible for sexual harassment. My face burned with shame as I pedaled my bike furiously, propelling myself away from him as fast as I could manage. After I arrived at church, I told the youth leader and a couple of others what happened. I remember saying, "I know it's not me, but it still makes me feel kind of dirty." I don't recall exactly what my youth leader and my friends said in return, but I remember their words focused on dismissing the man's actions. "Ugh, he's probably just a creepy old man. Don't worry about it."

I tried not to worry about it. And for the most part it didn't bother me, and I pushed the man out of my mind. I don't think I ever told my parents, even though the man had been right across the street and even though my dad would've employed every decibel of his commanding bass voice to ensure it never happened again. I was told not to worry, so I didn't. Still, somehow, I knew this wouldn't be the only time something like this happened to me. And I couldn't figure out why I felt so dirty—that part stuck.

I already had begun internalizing actions women take for safety when out in the world alone—holding my keys between my fingers when I walked through a parking lot and letting go of my bag if someone tried to grab it. I knew that some people thought less of me because I was a girl, and I knew that some people wanted to do things to me or hurt me because I had a female body. My friends and I never needed a self-defense course or a safety discussion to tell us that we were vulnerable. Somehow, we already knew. While I fretted about eventually getting my period and studied any images of breasts I could find in encyclopedias, magazines, and American Girl's *The Care and Keeping of You*, hoping to find an image of what I might look like someday, I also fretted about one day pumping my own gas at night. I worried about what would happen when I was independent, alone, and in possession of a woman's body. During the church service on the Sunday after the catcalling incident, I sang about Jesus and Father God and wondered if God had more in common with that rude man than with me.

By age twelve, I received lectures in youth group and summer camp, usually from men, about ensuring that my bra straps were covered and my shorts weren't too short. The youth leader issued a vague note to the girls about "not being a distraction to others." The boys in youth group received no directions on keeping their underwear bands covered, though they did receive some spotty instructions about removing their hats during prayers. I removed my hat too and was told that I didn't need to because I was a girl. Apparently, God didn't care about my hat—just my underwear.

In high school, I raced from volleyball games to youth group, still red-cheeked from exercise, and crawled into the back seat of my car to pull on sweatpants and a T-shirt to cover my uniform—the spandex shorts and racerback tank top that my pastor, youth pastor, and adult leaders saw me wear on the volleyball court as they cheered me on during a game. This outfit was fine on the court, but I would be chided and scowled at for wearing it in the fellowship hall. My church leaders praised my athletic accomplishments, but they could do this better when "it"—my pesky body—was covered. I quickly learned that the same people who were happy to support "me" had no trouble criticizing "it," using God as their reason for rebuke. I heard loud and clear from the church that God loved "me" and valued "me," but most of what God cared about with regard to "it" was about how "it" looked and how much of "it" could be seen. Over time, the space I created between "me" and "it" grew precipitously. It widened each time I was catcalled, each time I heard, "You'd be a great preacher if you weren't a girl," each time someone asked whether I wanted to work or have a family.

In churches and youth groups, at campgrounds and schoolyards, young women and girls hear—implicitly and explicitly—that their bodies are distractions and dangers. Once we cross into puberty, we may feel as though we have been handed a loaded gun with the safety off and told that we must never put it down, never point it at anyone else, and do everything in our power to ignore it while never lowering it for an instant. Later, when we try to take in the radical idea that we bear God's image, that we are beautiful reflections of God, that God glories in our creation, that *our bodies and their sensations matter to God*, the messages are deadened by decades of evidence to the contrary. These truths—ones that call us to imagine what it means that God *became flesh*—can't take root if we are working around-the-clock to master, tame, train, ignore, silence, or shrink our bodies.

Still, I know, beyond a shadow of a doubt, that bodies are important to God—because of the incredible, ridiculous, unbelievable story of the Incarnation. Right there in the Bible, in the midst of God doing mind-bendingly surprising, stupendous, nonsensical things like standing on the side of the poor and choosing murderers, slaves, scaredy-cats, and (gasp!) women as God's messengers, we find the Incarnation. The God of creation decides to place all God-self in a finite, carbon-based life-form: a body. God's best move—and a crazy intentional one at that—was to inhabit a body in order to demonstrate God's love, character, and work in the world. This act is the crux of our faith. Bodies are important to God. But how can we grasp the meaning of a fully embodied God when we don't know how to be fully embodied ourselves? How can we imagine the meaning of an embodied God when, for all our lives, we've been told that we are something separate and apart from our bodies?

The church's teachings on the body—and many other topics—have not been static throughout history. Church history is wild and glorious and, at times, completely bananas. It is filled with colorful characters and myths and agony and celebrations. It can feel like fan fiction that begins with something vaguely familiar and ends up somewhere entirely different than the Christianity we thought we knew. God may be steady and unchanging, but God's church is not. Because of how much the church's norms and ideals have formed cultures and systems—that is, the powers and principalities—and vice versa, some teachings, such as those surrounding women's roles in leadership, seem as though they may never change. But when viewed through the lens of church history, those teachings seem more fluid and dynamic. The church's radical view of women in its early days got lost and co-opted somewhere along the way. We overlook the stories of many women in scripture, though they dwell in the same pages as those of men. Not far from Noah lives Jael, not far from Samson lives Deborah, before Samuel there was his mother, Hannah. But their stories are not included with the universal childhood Bible stories of Adam, Noah, Moses, and David.

Anyone who has spent much time in Sunday school or vacation Bible school has learned songs and hand motions that go along with stories of Abraham (who had many sons), David (whose portrayal by Junior Asparagus in the Veggie Tales video *Dave and the Giant Pickle* sings, "Little guys can do big things too"), and Zacchaeus (the wee little man who climbed into a sycamore tree). Most of us don't learn songs about Jael and her tent spike, Deborah and her battle (surely just as important as the one Joshua fought at

Jericho), or Mary Magdalene. Over time, women's stories have been sidelined in our church teaching and preaching.

Growing up in church, I learned that certain bodies mattered to God, depending on what body you had. Male bodies were the default. Women's bodies? *Well*. Women's bodies didn't really come up, except with relation to modesty, sexual sins, temptation, and Mary. And even then, most of the time when we talked about Mary, we just talked about how she was a young girl or young woman when she had Jesus. Women's bodies were temptations (except in Mary's case), and women's sexuality was problematic (especially in Mary's case).[2]

Meanwhile, male bodies were frequently used as images of righteousness—usually by virtue of English translations using exclusively male pronouns to describe God's attributes, even in cases where the original language employed gender-neutral pronouns. For example, "The strength of *his* arm" (Luke 1:51, emphasis added) and the "armor of God," which is depicted framing a male body. (See Ephesians 6:10-18.) The only breasts to be found in the Bible, the only vivid imagery of women's bodies that I ever heard preached or taught, resided mostly in Song of Songs. And the church seemed to agree universally that this book of the Bible was the "sex text," only to be discussed during special retreats for teens.

Still, preachers and teachers always reminded us that God had a body, albeit one far more male than female, and that was one of the special things about Christianity. In perhaps the dead center of a Venn diagram of sweet Christian phrases and creepy Christian phrases lives an oft-repeated sentiment of pastors who call us to be "Jesus with skin on" to other people because we might be the only Jesus a person ever meets or knows. Ignoring the way that my mind linked this Christiany phrase to supernatural and sci-fi lore about skinwalkers, I understood what the speakers were trying to convey: It is our job as Christians to reveal Jesus to the world, to be God's hands and feet.

I know God had a body, and I know our bodies matter to God. But just as I know those things to be true, I also understand that *my* kind of body mattered less. God's Incarnation in Christ—this radical idea of God of Hosts presented as wholly enfleshed in a body like mine—never truly took hold in my life or my heart. In the context of church—especially after my child's body become a woman's body—I never knew what it felt like to be seen and honored while fully enfleshed in a body like mine.

In order to remain all-in during church, I—and many women like me—learned to dissociate. I wouldn't have called it that then, and I know many women who, though they agree with me, would still resist my word choice now. But I find it an apt descriptor. This habit formed from years of hearing "mankind" and "brothers" and "blessed is *he* who comes in the name of the Lord" and learning, without being told, that it was my job to mentally insert myself in each of those words, even though they didn't fit me, were never meant to fit me, would never be used to describe me outside the church, were not words I'd use to talk about myself.

I spent my time in church hearing male-specific pronouns for God, Jesus, and pretty much any other form of headship, even in a denomination that upheld women's spiritual leadership and ordination. God was synonymous with he/him/his and entirely separate from she/her/hers. And though I was told that this wasn't important, that of course we didn't think God Almighty was literally male, using female pronouns for God would turn God into a goddess, which was blasphemy because Christianity didn't believe in goddesses and because the God of the Bible was angered by goddess cults.

People in church shifted the way they interacted with me based on how womanly my body appeared and how much of that womanly body was visible to the naked eye at any given time. When my body shifted in that drastic journey from child to woman, the church weaponized it against me. The freedom of movement, of taking up space, of wearing whatever I liked (whether sloppy play clothes or highly dressed-up outfits) all slowly faded. Once I bore a woman's body, the church let me know I was a loaded gun, a distraction for all in my path. I could harm my brothers if I ever stopped paying attention. My body put me in danger, but I couldn't rid myself of it.

I learned to push myself away from my body and my woman's body in particular. Later, as I transitioned from a woman's body to a specifically mother's body, a new set of fears, expectations, and behaviors revealed themselves. Before I got pregnant and then, before pregnancy was noticeable, I feared the trappings that would automatically come with possessing a mother's body.

My first Sunday as a pregnant person was Mother's Day. Looking around at the women who were, in my opinion, "actual mothers," I was swept with a wave of dread. Would I be expected to receive with excitement and gratitude a bookmark covered in rosettes and a saccharine prayer written in gold calligraphy font? Would I be expected to give up hauling heavy tables and chairs around the sanctuary as I worked at the church? Would all my quirks, tastes, and hard-earned sense of identity disappear behind this new mantle of "mother," a role both venerated and invisible in the life of the church? Would I be relegated to serving in the nursery on a regular basis?

I was happy to be pregnant but ambivalent about becoming a mother. And the immediate demands for me to change my behavior—to remember prenatal vitamins and count milligrams of caffeine—made me recalcitrant about changing anything else I had control over. I felt sidelined by my own biological processes—the gulf between "me" and "my body" seemed to grow by the day. All I could do was ride it out. When I eventually shared news of my pregnancy with the wider world, my low-key excitement and ambivalence were noticeable. My friend Hallie finally took me aside and asked the question that, in hindsight, most people had probably wondered: "Are you okay? Was this pregnancy a surprise? Because it's okay if it was. It's a lot to handle."

"No," I said. "It's not a surprise. We did this to me on purpose. I just don't really know what to make of it. I can't begin to conceive of myself as a mother. All I can think of are all the things people are going to tell me I have to stop doing."

Though I did not realize it at the time, my attitude about pregnancy and motherhood was far from a singular experience. My friends—clergywomen, single women, married women, child-free women, mothers of miscarried children—identified with these same fears and anxieties. Many of us, I found, already felt weary from constantly blazing the path that allowed us to be who we were created and called to be. We were tired from continually re-asserting our full personhood—in the home, in the workplace, and in the body of Christ. Pregnancy and motherhood are hard enough without adding an extra identity to defend. They are hard enough without displaying our vulnerable wombs to the entire world. Moreover, I learned that our paths and worries—though new and our own—are also ancient and known.

The path was paved long before us by the many women in Jesus' lineage and again by the Marys, Martha, the unnamed woman at the well, the hemorrhaging woman, Tabitha, and so many more. And the path was continued and carried by the desert mothers—Amma Sarah, Amma Syncletica, Amma Theodora—and their mystic inheritors, the nuns of Helfta, Hildegard von Bingen, Bridget of Sweden, Julian of Norwich. This path, though frequently traveled and marked with signs helpful to its travelers, is swiftly overtaken by the creeping vines of the dark woods all around and sometimes eroded by torrents of vitriol at the same pace as new travelers can rebuild it.

Women's bodies—and the stereotypes and perceptions that come with them—have long been important to the life of the church. Even as women were forbidden from full ministerial authority, purportedly due to the sin of Eve and the writings of Paul, our bodies—flesh, blood, breasts, maternity, milk, and menopause—have been utilized as important and necessary images for how God interacts with the world, how we interact with God, and how we may best interact with and care for one another. Though we may suspect that women were the primary employers of female imagery, both for God and for explaining church and interpersonal interactions, the drivers of this phenomenon were male.

Starting in the second century, renowned church father Clement of Alexandria used the image of women's bodies nurturing children in-utero and nursing as a way of understanding the relationship and divine nutrition present in the Eucharist.[3] In addition to Clement, many early church writers including Origen, Augustine, and Saint John Chrysostom, on whose writings so much of both Western and Eastern Christianity are grounded, describe Jesus as a mother—not simply in metaphorical terms but with more literal images, calling for supplicants to nurse from the milk of Christ's breasts, nurse from the blood flowing from his side, or crawl into the wound in his side and be wholly supported and hidden there as a child in the womb.

Though this language rose and fell in popularity and usage over the centuries, the ways, wonders, and bodily experiences of women and mothers have been employed to enrich the life of the church. Unlike my experience in the contemporary church, where I learned implicitly that my woman's body was suspect, dangerous, and *almost never useful* as an analog for understanding how God works in the world, the historical church was happy to see God in women's bodies, especially in those functions that we currently hold as taboo—even as it continued to sideline women's leadership. Knowing now that Clement of Alexandria, far away in the second century, used the vivid imagery of maternal bodies and nursing women to draw his readers closer to the mystery of the Eucharist, I can't respond with anything but a wry smile when I remember how uncomfortable and fearful I was when I first nursed my baby in the middle of church.

Then as now, we are more comfortable with the images of mother's and women's bodies than we are with actual mothers and women, present, enfleshed, and whole, standing in front of us with heavy bellies and full breasts. Which begs these questions: Why are we more comfortable with our abstracted bodies than our actual ones? What have we lost by dissociating in order to participate in the church? What have we to gain by using our uniquely woman-bodied experiences to talk about God?

In many ways, I am not sure that we as Christians have spent enough time grappling with the Incarnation. What does it mean that we follow a God who emptied eons of

Divine Essence in order to walk the earth, confined to the same few pounds of flesh, sinew, and synapses? I am not sure we've contemplated, much less comprehended, what it means that God became fully vulnerable and dependent on us, the created. While our shared creeds that span the vast majority of Christendom hammer into us that Jesus was fully human *and* fully God, we still seem to spend more time in marvel at the fully God side of that equation. Unlike other systems of faith that feature embodied gods, Christianity is somewhat unique. Jesus did not begin as human and ascend, like Hercules, or begin Divine and descend as a fully formed, cognitively capable adult. We follow an Incarnate God, whose name is "God-with-us," and that "with" knows no bounds.

Understanding the process of fertility, pregnancy, birth, and nurturing an infant gives us a window into the radical, boundless vulnerabilities that our God chose to submit to. Though we'll never know all of Mary's unique journey in carrying the Christ child, we know that pregnancy itself is a vulnerable condition, during which countless things could go wrong for mother or child. God-with-us, we understand, is with us even to the point of vulnerability through failed conception, miscarriage, ectopic pregnancy, placenta previa, preeclampsia, incompetent cervix, maternal depression, vitamin deficiencies—the list is endless. Even so, God did not skip this treacherous, hurdle-filled process.

We follow a fully vulnerable God, who saw fit to participate completely in our way of being in the world—even through the utter dependence of a fetus, infant, and child.

We follow a God who had no qualms about being entirely encased by and dependent upon a human woman's body— not simply for the duration of the pregnancy but for the following year(s) as Mary's (or another woman's) body provided nourishment through nursing.

This flies in the face of most of the body-policing behaviors that surround women and mothers. If God entrusted the Divine Self wholly to a chosen servant, why do we feel compelled to put limits on the power and role of women in God's church? How, in a religion where God Incarnate was physically borne, supported, and raised by a woman, did we come to a place where women were seen as secondary to men in carrying the gospel? Why are women fit to carry God but not God's message? Why, if my female body is secondary, was it God's first and best choice? And why, if woman body and woman blood were adequate in God's sight to nurture the Savior, would women be somehow spiritually less adequate to preside over the remembrance of God's body and blood, poured out in sacrifice for God's children?

———

The wonder of the Incarnation is the wonder of creation, long separated from God's full presence, suddenly reunited. The wonder of Incarnation is that the same kind of flesh and blood that carries us was enough—in form and in value— to carry the Creator. Because the Creator loved and cared for and crafted our bodies so well that, broken and flawed and destined for death though we are, God still saw fit to choose to wear this skin. Because God chose to walk the world as Immanuel, as intimately with us as possible, we can understand that bodies matter to God. Bodies—including our wombs. Including the diseases that debilitate us, the feelings of brokenness that close our throats, the way feelings of fear can flood the heart and stomach. Bodies are important to God in a way that I did not contemplate until I found my own shifting, expanding, contracting in ways I did not control.

Bodies matter. Every body. All bodies.

And bodies break. Every body. All bodies.

And bodies rebuild.

Every body.

All bodies.

Even mine. Even yours.

CHAPTER 2

Prayer

Jesus took a loaf of bread, and after blessing it he broke it.
—Matthew 26:26

He stirs awake, first with tiny grunts, then with hands, arms, and feet flexing. The swaddle is broken; the warm comfort of the night gives way to cool need. His mouth opens, and his tongue pushes forward, his head nuzzling back and forth, searching for something to fill the empty. There is no thought, no judgment of the need, no pause to consider if now is a good time. There is just hunger—for nourishment or for comfort, for food or for warmth, there is no difference. They are bound together; they are the same.

The cry comes—wordless, urgent, wanting. *I need you. Hold me. Come, please come. I am not all right. I am empty or cold or scared of being alone. I'm not really sure, but they all feel the same to me. But come, please come.*

The needful cry may give way to greater anger, impatience, or urgency. The expression changes, but the impulse is the same. And then my arms find him, and he finds what I am offering. We are warm, body to body, heartbeat to heartbeat. His cries diminish, then vanish. My heart rate slows to normal, no longer quickened by the cry. We melt into the chair. I feel his body relax into mine. Rooted. Assured, with no doubt or second guess, that he is loved. Because at this point, all loved means is fed.

It is 3 a.m., 6 a.m., 9 a.m., noon, 3 p.m., 6 p.m., 9 p.m., midnight. Through need and nourishing, asking and providing, teaching and learning, together, again and again, we call and we answer. We pray the Hours.

————

I don't remember learning to pray to God; I remember praying to my grandfather.

My grandfather died when I was two years old—not old enough to remember him but old enough to pick up on my family's grief. I remember crying when alone in bed, praying to him but for what I wasn't sure. To make my mom feel better? To make me feel better? To let him know that I was sad he died? I recognize now that it was a child's way of connecting to undercurrents and emotions that were above my pay grade, things I could empathize with but not understand or articulate. My parents weren't into corporate prayer, whether at mealtime or bedtime. I believe they prayed, but it was something done in private.

Eventually, I learned that praying to God was the thing to do. The first formal lesson on prayer I remember receiving was in Ms. Vicki's fourth-grade Sunday school class. Ms. Vicki took us fourth-graders seriously even though we were children. She believed us when we had problems and took our concerns to heart without patronizing us. She wanted to hear our thoughts and opinions, and she encouraged us to ask questions about the Bible. Even still, Ms. Vicki had no problem chiding us and disciplining us. "There's a difference between acting like children and acting childish," she reminded us. "I encourage the first," she continued, "but I don't tolerate the second."

Seated at the Sunday-school table, sun pouring through the stained-glass windows, adding vibrant color to the sad, mottled carpet from the 1970s, Ms. Vicki taught us the correct format for prayer: A prayer should include thanks, intercession, petition, and gratitude. And always, *always*, in Jesus' name. That's where the power came from, she said. That phrase acted like a notary public; it made our prayer official and sent it *straight* to God. God was not a vending machine, Ms. Vicki insisted, but prayer did have a protocol. Prayer was a particular thing that one did or did not do, and the way we did it was important. Muslims prayed five times per day, with washing and bowing and kneeling. Our Catholic brothers and sisters prayed to saints. As Protestants, we prayed to God directly, and we could do it any time we wanted.

I appreciated Ms. Vicki's teachings. I believed that God wanted to hear from me—my thoughts, my concerns, my hopes—because Ms. Vicki showed me that she genuinely wanted to hear from me, even though I was a kid. So, when she said that prayer was talking to God and asking God for help, I believed her. She wouldn't steer me wrong. But like so much of our faith, there's more to it than what we glean from childhood. And like all things, our understanding of prayer must be allowed to grow.

———

I was first introduced to the Liturgy of the Hours at a Benedictine monastery in St. Meinrad, Indiana. There as a part of a capstone religion seminar during my senior year of college, I settled into sparse accommodations with a roommate and began to work. I'd brought one piece of homework and a few pieces of reading, some for pleasure but most required. I appreciated the respite from campus and was fascinated by the collective life of the monks there but had been apprehensive about how I would receive the silence and what I had perceived as a strict adherence to a schedule. As a tried-and-true ENFP on the Meyers-Briggs Type Indicator, I've never done well at getting myself to follow any sort of daily routine. Routine felt stifling and arbitrary, even if oftentimes necessary.

My introduction to the Hours left me feeling grounded, better in touch with myself, my work, and God. The regular interruptions to do something more important, more real than even my most pressing work, was freeing. I am prone to unproductive overwork, the sort where I may be so focused on a project that I forget to eat or drink but may have little to show for that effort. My focus, without grounding, yields only dribs and drabs of usable cohesive work and mostly piles of half-connected strands, an ever-growing amoeba of frayed strings at the edge of whatever I was attempting to weave together. But praying the Hours changed that. Instead of taking a deep breath and submerging myself until my lungs burned, the rhythm invited me to surface regularly to fill my lungs—not just with air but with the Spirit of God and God's work in the world. Praying the Hours represented my first taste of freedom through practicing discipline—and it was nothing short of intoxicating.

Similarly, I was not looking forward to the mundane routine of mothering a child through infancy. My mantra was that the key to happy parenting was basement-low expectations. When friends and loved ones would ask me what I was looking forward to about mothering a little one, I'd always have to pause. All my answers were activities you'd do with a four- or five-year-old, like going to the zoo or hiking. So I'd pause and then give a fake answer: "I can't wait to hold him" or "I'm so looking forward to putting socks on those teeny tiny feet."

Truthfully, I wasn't looking forward to any of that. I'd never been drawn to babies, never felt delight in holding them or caring for them. I enjoyed preschoolers and grade-school children—persons who could talk to me and play pretend and let me see inside their amazing, creative minds. But infants? *No.* I had very low expectations of what I thought of as the "crying potato" phase. I fully expected to do nothing other than grit my teeth and get through the first year by sheer willpower.

When the time came for the constant, regular inter-ruptions of feeding an infant, I was amazed at my response. It didn't feel like work; it felt like praying the Hours. Both called me out of myself, grounding me in a greater reality than whatever I was working on. I wondered if the ancient monks understood that their waking to attend to prayer was so fundamentally close to the waking of mothers, that the rhythm they'd chosen mirrored the expected and taken-for-granted work of mothers in their world.

Since the time of the early monastics, praying the Hours—that is, interrupting daily life at set times each day to connect with the Divine through set pauses and ritu-als—has been a discipline of faith. Many churches continue to hold between one and four daily prayer services during the week. The Episcopal Book of Common Prayer, used for individual and corporate practice by many Christians, contains services for Morning, Afternoon, Vespers, and Compline Prayers. Monastic communities commonly build between three and seven prayer pauses into the day. In Islam, our Muslim siblings pause for prayer five times dur-ing the day. Jewish prayer books contain prayers for both set times of the day and regular daily tasks, such as entering a doorway or cooking a meal. The fact remains that most ways that we have found to relate with the Divine have included frequent check-ins and daily pauses to ground ourselves in nourishment and relationship. Christians are no different, and our special emphasis on God as Immanuel, "God with us," gives rise to our belief that we may access God anywhere, any time. God is never too far, never out of hearing range of our cries and calls for connection.

Though our ancient traditions have always pointed to this, I, like many others, was taught that prayer is a specific action, requiring a certain form, attitude, or content in order to count as prayer. At the very least, we learn from scripture that prayer often looks like a person turning his or her attention to God with a request: "Answer me when I call, O God" (Ps. 4:1) or "Now therefore, O our God, listen to the prayer of your servant and to his supplication" (Dan. 9:17). Many who attend church as children are taught guides for prayer like the one Ms. Vicki taught me—praise, thanks, ask, intercession, submission, in Jesus' name, Amen. In other Christian traditions, prayer is thoroughly covered as a part of catechism or confirmation classes. Either way, we may find ourselves left with the equivalent of a solicitation call script if we are not careful. *Hey, God! How are things going for you today? Great to hear. Listen, I'm so thankful you took the time to talk to me today. And I have an offer—nay, an opportunity!— for you to bless me. If my request doesn't take too much of your time and would guarantee I wouldn't need to bother you again for at least another six months, would you be interested in helping me get this job today? Thanks so much. In Jesus' name. Amen.*

For those of us who turn to faith in adulthood or perhaps more informally throughout our lives, prayer may seem a bit more mysterious—something that seems to spontaneously erupt from us in times of great trouble or uncertainty. In the tradition of praying the Hours, however, much of the work of prayer is accomplished through presence and intention. Prayer begins not with the opening lines of a liturgy or with the sound of the bells; it begins in the rising. The words, the form, the psalms, and service are the framework that our prayers may hang upon, but the prayer itself begins with our coming into the presence of God and allowing ourselves to set aside our material reality for the true kingdom of God.

Like the unrelenting cries of a hungry infant, the Hours call us to experience the urgency of God's work in the world. And like the rhythm and practice of feeding a child, the work is both urgent and never-ending. It will repeat—sometimes sooner than we would like. Prayer, like nourishing another person, may demand more of us than we had planned to offer. The endless early hours of feeding my son during his first year of life awakened me to a new posture of prayer. As his cries grew sharper, his need more deeply felt, his desperation and alarm climbing higher, I found myself cooing, "It's all right, sweetheart. I'm right here." Or, in less magnanimous moments, "Geez, kid! I am literally right here. Can you give me just one second to unlatch my bra? Take a deep breath!"

This rhythm and newfound role gave me room to experience prayer—that desire for nourishment and shared

presence—from the perspective of the Divine. I heard
anew the voice of God saying, "I have never been far from
you. If only you would turn and hear my voice, I could
solve your troubles." I felt the mutuality of the prayer and
presence relationship. Knowing that as I was created in the
image of God, I could catch glimpses of God's true character through myself and the act of feeding a child. I know
now that when my child is nourished, I too benefit—either
because my breasts are painful and aching to be drained or
because my heartbeat slows and settles as he relaxes into
me with a bottle. Just as God created us to be in relationship with God, I see now that God is happier, God's heart is
"gladdened" when we allow our overtired, cranky, hungry,
overstimulated selves to relax into God's presence. And in
whatever way we come to God—kicking and screaming,
quietly mewling, half-asleep, or in the middle of play—
God's response will be always the same. God will offer
nourishment, presence, and arms ever-ready to encircle,
even if they are met with kicking, biting, and pushing away.
Even if we bite at the most sensitive, vulnerable parts God
has to offer, they will be made available to us again. And
eventually we will fall into the rhythm of a shared life, of
calling and answering, of mutual need and meeting.

Late-night feedings don't begin when the nipple makes
contact with a child's mouth; they begin with the rising.
Though our babe may not know it for several minutes, we
respond as soon as we are able. Prayer begins with the rising. The moment we turn ourselves to God, God—like a

mother—begins turning toward us, even if we may not see or feel God's presence for some time.

It is no accident, I think, that the Lord's Prayer and Eucharist are tied together—no accident that we remember how God taught us to pray during the same ritual we use to remember how God feeds through God's body, nourishes through God's blood. Just as male metaphor has been used for thousands of years to understand God, so too does a female understanding of God put flesh on and allow us to wrap our fingers around an abstract, too-big-to-comprehend truth. The female body can feed through body (via nursing) and nourish through blood (via placenta). When we see this about ourselves, we are given a new gateway with which to encounter and understand God. The early church found these two practices vital to the Christian faith, vital enough that they formed the core of what eventually became the rhythm of our weekly church services: prayer (founded upon the Lord's Prayer), proclamation of the Word, baptism (birth and rebirth through water), and Communion (feeding and nourishing ourselves through the body of God). I can't help but see the care of a mother reflected in our church services, that while she feeds, she tells stories and she sings.

Praying the Hours, like feeding newborns, is a holy interruption. And I don't say this to over-sanctify the difficult work of feeding newborns. If we're sleepless and bleary-eyed, if our nipples are cracked and bleeding, if it's 4 a.m. and the bottle warmer bites the dust, if our child struggles to eat or struggles to keep what he or she eats in his or her body—it is a slog. It is painful. It is difficult. And it may not feel holy, but none of the struggles diminishes its holiness. Through caring for children, we open ourselves to the possibility of transformation—of seeing our daily work in alignment with spiritual discipline, of recalling that what matters most is that we feed each other and let ourselves be fed, that we allow ourselves to settle into the presence of ones that care for us and accept what they offer.

In the church, before the Lord's Prayer, many of us recite this sentence: "Let us pray as Jesus taught his disciples to pray." Just as Jesus explicitly teaches us how to serve one another when he washes the disciples' feet and how to feed one another and transform the world through our care, so does Jesus teach us to pray. Not in an elaborate scheme, not in a particular place, time, or attitude, but as a child asking a parent for food, forgiveness, and a place to be held.

CHAPTER 3

Breaking, Giving & Sacrificing

On the night [Jesus] was handed over to suffering and death, our Lord Jesus Christ took bread; and when he had given thanks to you, he broke it, and gave it to his disciples, and said, "Take, eat: This is my Body, which is given for you. Do this for the remembrance of me."

—The Book of Common Prayer,
The Holy Eucharist: Rite Two

I received from the Lord that which I also delivered to you: that the Lord Jesus on the same night in which He was betrayed took bread; and when He had given thanks, He broke it and said, "Take, eat; this is My body which is broken for you; do this in remembrance of Me."

—1 Corinthians 11:23-25, NKJV

No matter how we are born, no matter how we birth, we all begin with breaking. The womb gives way to the world, and the world it contained breaks apart, falls away. The mother-bodies that bore us up to that point, shifting their organs while weaving ours, break and give way in one final act of carrying. Whether born into death or into life, no matter how many weeks' gestation— the breaking is ever-present. It is inescapable. Though the breaking is an unavoidable part of our human condition, it surprises us, leaving us gasping and breathless. We know we must break, but we are unsure how to break well.

A week after my son was born, I awakened alone. He was still in the Neonatal Intensive Care Unit (NICU), not yet ready to tolerate life outside my body without significant support. My body, on the other hand, was ready to feed him round the clock. So at 3 a.m., I found myself nursing a breast pump instead of a tiny partner. After twenty minutes of the hard work of juggling flanges, dials, and tubes and then finding a way to relax enough to let down, I rose to complete the ritual washing of the equipment.

Glancing at myself in the bathroom mirror, I laughed. I felt like myself, but the reflection I saw was new—same body, entirely different form. Long hair barely held in a low ponytail, hormonal cystic acne spread across my face, neck, and upper chest. Breasts achingly swollen even though I'd just completed pumping. Abdomen rumpled by the hard outline of the binder support the hospital had provided for my post-C-section healing. Eyes heavy and bleary with the lateness of the hour. My face, arms, and fingers were visibly puffy, both from the postpartum hormones and from my preeclamptic blood pressure, which remained high for a few weeks after my son's birth. Milky suds, tinged Palmolive green, rushed down the sink as I studied myself. *So this is my body*, I thought.

At the same time, I heard the distant echo of celebrants and officiants, pastors and preachers at the Common Table, reciting the Communion liturgy: "This is my body, broken for you. This is my blood, shed for you." In that moment, my relationship to myself, to the church, and to Christ shifted. The words that I'd regarded as symbols of death and sacrifice resounded in my ears as ones that applied to birth and life. This *was* my body. It *was* my blood. Broken, shedding, a necessary component of the process of bringing new life into the world. The breaking and bleeding hadn't killed me, though they threatened to; instead, they had transformed me. Breaking was the starting point for a brand-new life. How had I never noticed that bodies given and blood shed are not relegated to the Communion table but instead are the exact manner through which we are all brought to life? And why hadn't I ever heard my pastors, preachers, and teachers make that connection?

Even though we come into this world through breaking and giving and even though we all leave our bodies when we're too broken to sustain life, we have little knowledge at the outset about what these actions mean or require. In other words, we are not born knowing how to birth; we are not born knowing how to die. Though women's bodies were created to allow labor and birth to occur, we invest lots of time, thought, and energy into learning how to do this work well. Labor classes, doulas, birth coaches—we've built an industry around teaching gestational parents and mothers how to do that which, in theory, our bodies were designed to carry out with a moderate amount of success with little or no intervention. But though we were designed to birth, not even thousands of years of evolutionary processes have managed to create a *safe* birth. We may have evidence that our bodies instinctively know how to birth, but we have none that indicates that we instinctively know how to survive that process. So we take classes on how to break well, how to live through the breaking, how to prepare for something that human history has depended on—even as we skirt past the details and specifics in polite company.

Birth is an intensely personal experience for the birther and those closest to her, and many of us find sharing our most profound life experiences with others to be difficult. But our discomfort and distance from birth and female bodies has left us with a language deficit. Not only do we struggle to talk about birth because of its intense nature, but also we struggle to find spaces where that talk is acceptable. Even once that space is afforded, we often find that we come up short. What words do we have for describing the combination of joy, utter terror, crippling depression, and feelings of dysphoria experienced by women in the days leading up to and following birth? We frequently infantilize those feelings with the term *baby blues*, which only serves to downplay and dismiss the intensity of postpartum experiences.

In the days after I gave birth, I struggled to understand myself or explain what was happening to me physically, emotionally, and psychologically. I wrote, prayed, drew, and breathed. Some friends helped me find handholds. Joanna, a daughter of an immigrant father, said, "You're still the same person, but you're in a radically different place now—in a foreign country almost. It's okay if you feel like you've lost your bearings. You haven't done this before, and the learning curve is high. It's okay to feel lost, and it's okay to keep speaking the language you knew in your homeland. You'll adjust in time." Her gift of words gave me a way to understand myself and to try explaining my feelings of displacement to others. A friend from an online community gave me another handhold. She'd given birth a few weeks before I did, and her experience also included preeclampsia and a stint in the NICU for her baby. She said, "I remember feeling as though I'd been slowly sucked out of my own body and then shoved into a second-rate copy. It was like living in a knockoff Louis Vuitton."

In the worst of times, no standard English words could do the job. Leaving my son in the hospital three days after his birth, driving home with an empty car seat, and hugging a giant rented breast pump rather than a baby sent me reaching into language from J. K. Rowling's magical universe of the Harry Potter series. The only word that sufficed was a made-up one: *splinched*. *Splinching* occurs when a witch or wizard fails to *disapparate* (magically teleport) completely. A body part—a leg, a finger, an eyebrow—is cut off from the body and left behind in the place they'd *disapparated* from. The pain and reality of driving home, leaving my tiny child who until recently had been a very important part of my own body, could only be captured in this word.

If we are to carry our own experiences and those of others, we must learn to talk about uncomfortable things. In my case, in the days leading up to my son's birth, I had to find the words to tell my husband that if I were incapacitated and the care team told him he had to choose who to save—me or the baby—I still wanted him to choose me. They weren't words I was prepared for or feelings anyone talked about. They're still not words I share or say aloud very often. But with all hard things, it gets easier with practice. Naming our experiences—even the uncomfortable, difficult, and heart-wrenching ones—is the practice we need to be able to fully embrace what happens to us. We must practice breaking and birthing.

One of the first things I heard in a birthing class was that pain is part of the process; it's not something we have to fear. The pain of contractions is a side effect of our body doing exactly what it should be doing, and our sensations of that pain are a signal of how labor is progressing. Some methods strive to realign our understanding of the birth process by eliminating the language of *pain* and *contraction* from their birth vocabulary; instead, they focus on *pressure, waves,* and other alternate terms for describing the body's work in labor and the discomfort associated with it. Either way, pain or pressure are inescapable. They are part and parcel of bringing new life into the world.

Pain happens when we turn our insides out, delivering a baby and an extra organ that had, until moments prior, been woven into our being. Pain is awful, but it is important and manageable. It lets us know when it is time to break and how well we are healing. In birth classes, teachers invite us to view ourselves as flowers opening to the world, channels of gulf-stream currents, or skiers riding a massive avalanche as it courses down a mountainside. They remind us again and again that this pain is not a symptom of death but a pathway toward what's to come. And while some of us labor through many hours of pain, some only few, and some experience pain differently—say, the pain associated with a spinal block and a C-section—we all find that the only way *around* is *through*. Despite what the marketers say, we do not yet have the technology to have a truly "pain-free birth." (I wish I would've known that before I spent hours falling down endless YouTube rabbit holes.) And the *through* part of birth is almost universally felt as a deathlike process until we learn to reframe our relationship to the pain. As we birth, we often catch a glimpse of death—we feel as though we are going to die or that a complication may incapacitate us. In the intense moments of birth, most women describe feeling as though they are close to death. Death and life, it seems, are not strangers. And though not all of us birth, we all must learn to die.

———

In monastic communities—that is, those cloistered communities based on ancient Christian texts and spiritual practices—meditations on death and mortality are woven into daily life and observance. Prayers concluding the day, often known as Compline, read, "May almighty God grant us a peaceful night and a perfect end. Amen" (BCP). Each evening, before closing the day, monks and nuns around the world reflect on their eventual death. They pray for it. They practice acknowledging death and preparing for its eventual arrival.

Needless to say, this is not a common practice for the rest of us. It is not glamorous and not likely to follow on the heels of hot yoga or mindful coloring as the cool new spiritual practice. And even if it were, it's not the kind of mindfulness habit that one brings up at a dinner party. Imagine smiling over petit-fours as Jeff from accounting shares how yoga has changed his life, listening to Martha as she shares her prayer and meditation practice, and then adding to the conversation, "If you like that stuff, you should try my practice. I meditate on my inevitable death each night before bed." Our fellow partygoers would be as thrilled to hear about our death meditations as they would to hear about our colon cleanse. But even if they are unpopular fodder for dinner-party conversations, these processes of birth and death, breaking open into another side of life that we've only vaguely been able to comprehend, provide us with much-needed practice for this business of surviving our own lives.

This dinner-party image reminds me of Jesus sitting at a table with his friends at Passover, celebrating the deliverance of God's people. Yes, he celebrates the national festival of an occupied people, but he also enjoys a family feast. Jesus has collected and carried his disciples through the world for years, but now—as scripture tells us—Jesus knows his time is coming. The new world bulges out of the womb, the skin of the world tightening, ready to give way to what is to come. And it is Jesus' work to offer one final act of carrying; it is his work to break open. I wonder if Jesus is practicing his labor during the Last Supper. Instead of Lamaze or the Bradley Method, Jesus pulls his closest friends around him and lays out the plan. No birthing soundtrack, no lovingly selected items brought from home, no birth plan. Just the sound of dishes and cups clanging on a table, chewing, laughing, praying, and talking. Breathing in and breathing out, grounding himself in the path that lies ahead for the next two days. Early labor. The already but not yet. The urgency and the waiting. The pain that comes before the new life emerges.

We can't know Jesus' thoughts for certain, but we know that his isn't a story of serene acceptance and surrender to the pain that is to come. At least, not at first. After the Last Supper, Jesus retreats with his friends—his chosen family— to Gethsemane, where he asks them to keep watch with him while he prays through the night. The scriptures describe him wracked with distress, sweating blood and crying. And as his body shudders under the pressure, he cries out to God, "My Father, if it is possible, let this cup pass from me; yet not what I want but what you want" (Matt. 26:39). Even Jesus, God-with-us, struggles with the pain of death, the pressure of breaking in order to allow the New Covenant to give way. Suffering, though embedded in our life experiences, does not come easily. Yet even God understands.

I don't know why breaking is the admission price that we pay for access to life, but I take comfort in the fact that I follow a God who is intimately in touch with the process. A God who knows that brokenness doesn't always leave visible bruises, even as our bodies crumble under devastating, unseen wounds. A God who knows that families formed by choice are important and valid, even though these families acknowledge loss. Just as we follow a God who understands our physical sufferings, so too do we have an example of how God values families born of choice, grief, and loss. We cannot confine motherhood to pregnancy and birth. Breaking and sacrificing are not confined to waters and wombs.

Just as we recognize the work of birth in Jesus' experience of suffering in his body, scripture tells us that Jesus likewise recognizes that families are made by choice and need, loss and grief. In John 19:26-27, in the midst of grief, loss, and uncertainty, Jesus sees the importance of forming a new family: "When Jesus saw his mother and the disciple whom he loved standing beside her, he said to his mother, 'Woman, here is your son.' Then he said to the disciple, 'Here is your mother.' And from that hour the disciple took her into his own home." At this moment, Jesus creates a different kind of family—a family that didn't look like others, a family that was accustomed to grief and loss as companions on the journey.

However we form our families and however our families are broken and rebuilt over the course of our lives, the process takes courage. Family members grow and pass away, taking what they need from us and leaving familiar but strange reflections behind. Our mothered bodies are shaped beneath the hands that birthed us, hands that cared for us, and hands that bore us up where others would crush. Our mothering bodies creak and strain, holding up the full weight of sick children, bearing up under a joyful dog pile, or stretching to hold onto family ties we'd never choose but are ours just the same. Bodies given, bodies received, bodies given again, all in remembrance and testimony that though pain is part of the path, something loved and new lives on the other side.

Learning to break, to die, to give, and to let our whole worlds give way to something new and unknown is an unavoidable part of life—unavoidable but often hidden. We gloss over the pain and dysphoria of birth and postpartum life. We mourn silently when others assume we're "dragging our feet" about having children when in reality we're in the throes of fertility treatments and multiple miscarriages. We often do not speak about the devastation of divorce or the loss at the center of adoption. Somewhere along the way we lose the ability to name pain, death, and suffering for what they are. And when we cannot name them, we struggle to own our experiences as we go through them. Our breaking is inevitable, but, thankfully, so is our resurrection. As we practice breaking, we practice birthing. We practice the process that leads us to life.

CHAPTER 4

Blood

"This cup is the new covenant in my blood,
which is poured out for you."

—Luke 22:20, NIV

Blood. Wet blood, dry blood, bloody blood. Brown or pink or deep, rushing red. We burst forth from our mother's bodies covered in it. It's drained from us after we die. Regardless of our personal feelings on the matter, our lives are measured in blood. To be embodied is to be born in blood. No exceptions—not even for God. And for those of us who menstruate, we measure our lives, both medically and materially, through blood. Menarche. Menses. Pre-menstrual. Menstrual. Post-menstrual. Last menstrual period. Perimenopause. Menopause. Amenorrhea.

Oligomenorrhea. Menorrhagia. The "before" time—all the time before our first period. The "after" time—after our periods are finished, our bodies stop their blood flow (however routine or unpredictable it may have been).

We measure our lives in other befores and afters and the times in-between: The time before our first pregnancy. The time after our first miscarriage. The time before cancer or after diagnosis. The time when an illness stopped our bleeding or the time our bleeding was healed. The time between our last real period and its eventual return post-pregnancy. The time a rude boyfriend dismisses our bad mood by ascribing it to PMS. The time we struggle to explain the reason for our medical absence due to the pain of a burst ovarian cyst or endometriosis. The time our care provider asks the date of our last period and we pause, scrambling for our calendars, wondering how bleeding for days is so normal that it's forgettable.

———

My Sunday school teachers taught me sanitized stories from the Old Testament. Noah's Ark, David and Goliath, and Jonah and the whale all appeared on worn flannel boards in the nursery. We sang about Jesus' blood at church, and, at some point, I understood that he died but wasn't really dead. The only blood we ever talked about in detail was during Communion and when we talked about Cain and Abel. Stories of death and blood unsettle us, even as we follow a faith with a central ritual of that includes both. I was taught that the first human bloodshed was Abel's, when his jealous brother Cain killed him. But I've had that story wrong my entire life.

The Bible is bloody. This is a fact about which none of us disagree. Though Christians of various denominations and faith traditions diverge on many matters, we can agree that our holy scriptures are full of blood, death, and dismemberment. From Cain and Abel to the books of Kings and the Crucifixion, the stories of our faith tell of blood being spilt. But the first time one human spilled another's blood did indeed involve Cain, but Abel wasn't even there—Eve was.

Though we often overlook this part of the story, the first blood spilled on the planet wasn't spilled in murder; it gushed forth in life. Eve's blood first stained the soil—not Abel's. It spilled during agony and then elation. Remembering that Eve was the first person to bleed changes the way we understand ourselves as God's people. Our sense of where we come from shapes who we are. Skipping Cain's birth and jumping straight to Abel's death means we miss the fruit that comes from holding our innocence in tension with our greed. We miss out on a miracle—after all, when was the last time we stopped to ponder what it must have been like for that very first woman to bear the very first baby? When we skip Eve's blood, we start the trend of skipping major parts of the story—especially if they have to do with bodies and their icky processes.

Even before our first periods, we are both fascinated and horrified by the process. We fill locker rooms and recess huddles with questions—Will it hurt? What does it feel like? Will we feel any different afterward? Young-adult author Judy Blume made a fortune writing to this audience's fear and fascination. Blood makes us uncomfortable. Whether between the onionskin pages of our Bibles or a sudden appearance on a bedsheet, bloody episodes—though the most human of all—are met with squeamishness. We do anything to distance ourselves—from ignoring Jael and her tent spike (see Judges 4:17-22) to using euphemisms for getting our period. Even when we approach the Passion and the Common Table, we both desire to draw closer to God and want to keep our distance from all that blood. Most of us approach with less caution when asked to eat bread as Christ's body. Thanks to the abundance of metaphor and recent spates of young-adult literature about vampires, we still, if given a moment of reflection, shudder a bit while drinking the cup.

The early church fathers and mothers shared this impulse to distance themselves from the bloody portions of the story, though they focused on sanitizing Jesus' birth rather than his death. Though crucifixes and holy art grew bloodier, the birth of Jesus—and Mary's role in it—were gradually made a hemoglobin-free zone. Far from the labor and birth that the rest of us know, the baby Jesus comes to us in a bloodless, silent manger, surrounded by adoring animals and Joseph, standing off, alone.

As a clueless Protestant, I never knew what to make of Mary. In youth groups, she was presented as a girl—fourteen or so—and offered as an example of how God can use young women to change the world. Of course, like Mary, that would only be possible if we were chaste. After all, God didn't pick a harlot for Jesus' mother, so that was supposed to tell us something. Later, I came to know her as the maiden Mary or the Virgin Mary. As I grew older than her age at the Annunciation, the church's focus and messages about Mary shifted to her faith, her deference to God, and her celibacy—especially her celibacy.

Eventually, I began to hear about Mary as courageous, brave, even revolutionary. Comparing the Magnificat to a protest song, Mary came to life as a thinking, astute young woman who was shaped by the God of her scriptures—a God who favored the poor and fed the hungry but sent the rich away empty all for righteousness's sake. Even so, Mary, Mother of God, a young woman of serious faith, felt as distant from me as an extraterrestrial. I could relate well to Peter, famous for loudly saying the wrong thing and for abandoning his friends when the going got tough. I even could relate to the father who pleads, "I believe; help my unbelief!" (Mark 9:24). But Mary was an afterthought, a backdrop, a statue. Though she was a young woman who strove to serve God—in many respects the closest connection I could have to a biblical character—she was entirely other. And once I was no longer a virgin, Mary and I had one fewer thing in common.

Catholic and Orthodox traditions venerate Mary, and their devotion has lasted for centuries and reveals a lot about our views of Mary. Mary's blessedness transformed her into a superhuman. Or, perhaps, a nonhuman. Mary was special not only because she carried Jesus but also because her very body was stripped of all the problematic parts of pregnancy and motherhood. Turns out, our church fathers and mothers were just as uncomfortable with the bloodiness of birth as we tend to be. They considered red blood unclean, with menstrual blood being especially ghastly. As the Christian church took root in the early centuries CE, other Hebrew-speakers commonly hurled insults at Christian followers, accusing them of being devoted to a *ben niddah*, a child conceived of a menstruating woman. This was one of the nastiest curses and slurs in the language, rooted in the fundamental belief that blood was deeply unclean and bleeding women the same by extension.[4] From this environment, rather than imagine an angle in which the Incarnate God participated in or passed through that very blood, our forebears decided that Mary couldn't have normal blood. Instead, they decided Mary's blood was white.[5]

To further place Mary on an unreachable maternal pedestal, many theologians discussed the state of her uterus. According to Saint Bridget of Sweden, Mary's uterus "shines, containing as it does the divine child: her womb 'was as perfectly clean as ivory and shone like a place built of exquisite stones.' The walls 'were like the brightest gold.'"[6] In the words of German mystic Gertrude of Helfta, Mary's womb was "'as transparent as the purest crystal' and that her 'internal organs, penetrated and filled with divinity,' shine brightly, 'just as gold, wrapped in silk of various colours, shines through a crystal.'"[7]

Eve, cursed as she was, couldn't have any part in God passing into the mortal coil. So her labor pains could never visit Mary since that would imply that Mary was under the mantle of sin and, thus, Jesus would be tainted by the sin of Mary's blood or pain. So theologians stripped Mary of her labor with the Christ child. Instead, according to *The Catechism of the Council of Trent*, Jesus arrived "just as the rays of the sun penetrate without breaking or injuring in the least the solid substance of glass, so after a like but more exalted manner did Jesus Christ come forth from His mother's womb without injury to her maternal virginity."[8] And if the ray of light analogy doesn't seem plausible, we turn to Hildegard von Bingen, who asserted that Mary went to sleep in the manger and woke with a shock when "'the infant came forth from her side—not from the opening of the womb—without her knowledge and without pain, corruption, or filth.'"[9] For good measure, Bridget of Sweden asserts that "the Virgin's womb, which before the birth had been very swollen, at once retracted; and her body then looked wonderfully beautiful and delicate."[10]

When we consider Mary, we think of anything and everything but a birth. We do not speak of blood loss, midwives, a placenta, or afterbirth. When we sing and pray on Christmas Eve, we picture a cleaned, swaddled newborn and happy, tired parents. We take away every difficult, "icky" portion of God's journey to become flesh and insert a jewel-studded uterus and a clean baby. In our collective efforts to venerate Mary, we undo the very work that gave her a front-row seat at the miracle of miracles. We make her a bystander—and a nonhuman bystander at that. If we don't have room within our worshiping communities to ponder the visceral mysteries of God's birth in the world, no wonder we struggle to make room for our own difficult, bloody, and holy moments.

That's the tricky thing about veneration. It can disconnect us from the object of our adoration. It can minimize the humanity of the venerated. We no longer recognize ourselves in the thing we call holy. We gild the lily, and we take it so far that other lilies no longer feel worthy of the name. I don't believe for a second that our smart, stalwart, faithful sisters Bridget, Gertrude, and Hildegard sought to push Mary away from us or distance the embodied God-child from the miracle of Incarnation. I know, having read their words and found myself in them, that God was present and working in their lives just as in my own. But at the same time, I can't help but shake my head at what's come to pass. Gertrude and her crew got the ball rolling with the idea that a body springing back to pre-baby form is a sign of God's favor or a woman's worth.

Protestants, though free from some of the trappings that make Mary unreachable, have our own problems. Mary is forgotten, seldom pondered, and often portrayed in ways that emphasize her as meek, humble, and submissive. When she is acknowledged at all, it is only as Jesus' mother. While Protestants may balk Mary's veneration, Catholic and Orthodox believers may balk at Protestants' utter lack of acknowledgment or time spent marveling at the priestly work accomplished by Mary as Theotokos, "the Bearer of God."

No matter how we approach her, Mary's work—her willingness to endure ridicule, hardship, bodily discomfort, and distress; her blood and her body and her nurturing of God-Incarnate while he threw food and tantrums and then turned to bury himself in her skirts—stands as a testament that all this invisible labor is seen, noted, and valued by God. Not just in an abstract way that puts motherhood on a pedestal but up close, real, and, raw.

———

Carrying a child during the month of December turned my attention to Mary. Instead of a silent background piece to the Nativity, as I'd always seen her portrayed, Mary suddenly felt close at hand. A lover of all things Advent, I was thrilled when I realized my due date would have me swollen large during the Christmas season. By June, I had already asked my pastor if I could have dibs on reading some Mary or Elizabeth passages as liturgist in the coming season. The idea of reading their words excited me, at last giving me a connection to these radical women who felt so untouchable. As life had it, though, I wasn't in church once during the Advent of my pregnancy.

At Thanksgiving celebrations with my family, two and a half hours from my preferred hospital, I stood up to get a slice of my grandmother's apple pie and knew immediately that something wasn't right. I experienced that same horror that I had known since junior high: standing up after a long spell of sitting, only to be seized by the knowledge that I most certainly was bleeding through my pants. But this time, my worry carried additional terror. Something was wrong, very wrong. I saw red everywhere—too much, too fast. I was too far from the hospital and two months too early.

As my husband sped down country highways, suddenly Mary was all I could think about. Mary, who swayed on a donkey and hoped not to go into labor on her journey, while I jolted and bled more with every poorly patched pothole on IL-67. Mary, who gave birth in a manger, while I was afraid of losing a baby beside a car in a cow pasture. Though my Protestant suspicion of Mary kept her at arm's length, she suddenly became a figure of comfort. The language and stories I'd been given for times of distress weren't adequate, and they fell away like brittle rungs on a ladder when I tried to pull myself out of a pit of pain and fear. Joshua at Jericho didn't offer comfort; I wasn't battling a foreign enemy. Other stories I loved for their wisdom and revelation about how God works in the world didn't seem to apply. I didn't need Moses' call or Abraham's reckless faith or Peter's steadfast witness. I didn't need parted waters or burning bushes. I needed a birth story and a birthing body. I needed a Mary who was human like me. I needed a laboring Mary, breathing through Braxton Hicks contractions on the way to Jerusalem with a nervous Joseph by her side.

And Mary delivered.

God cares about the work of mothers—not because being a mother is a woman's place or highest calling or biological imperative—because in, with, and through our bodies, God Almighty created, met, and redeemed us for the salvation of the world. Our bodies and blood were sufficient to carry God into the world and to create pathways for others to connect with God when all other avenues fell short. Our bodies are so radically enough that God entered the world—through flesh, bone, blood, amniotic fluid, placenta, and vernix—to prove God's love for us. When we marvel at the Incarnation, the Nativity, and the Common Table, we remember that we follow an Almighty God who saw fit to become wholly vulnerable and dependent on God's creation—specifically, dependent on the body of a young woman who, in her culture and time, was raised to believe her body was the property of her father and future husband. Even so, consulting neither, God came directly to her. And she, consulting neither, said yes. Though hidden or uncomfortable or taboo, our bodies and blood tell the story of God as long as we are willing to pay attention.

CHAPTER 5

Being Consumed

*Take them in remembrance that Christ died for you,
and feed on him in your hearts by faith,
with thanksgiving.*
—The Book of Common Prayer,
Holy Eucharist: Rite Two

*Take this, all of you, and eat of it,
for this is my Body . . .
Take this, all of you, and drink of it,
for this is my Blood.*
—Order of Mass, Eucharistic Prayer I

Christ strives to eliminate the space between himself and others, surrendering entirely to us and offering his body and blood to be consumed over and over and over again. Such is the luxury of a limitless, metaphysical being. I, on the other hand, am finite and have boundaries. In their earliest days, infants cannot conceive of a separation between themselves and their mothers. Worse yet, many mothers can't conceive of one either. The child acts like a drowning person who desperately clings to his or her rescuer, pushing his or her mother underwater and holding her there without realizing the trouble that makes for both of them.

I elected to breastfeed, and my body allowed me to do so. After fighting my body for the final weeks of a pre-eclamptic pregnancy, my ability to produce a never-ending milk supply at only thirty-four weeks of gestation was a miracle to me. On the night of my son's birth, separated due to our differing medical needs, I remember marveling at the fact that I easily pumped breast milk. For the remainder of my son's hospitalization, I held a standing appointment with my pump every three hours. I received confusing advice from lactation specialists that I should pump until I was empty, but I found that I never was. Somehow, some way, there was always more.

This began my first lesson in motherhood, which helped to assuage the fears I had during my pregnancy. Before the urine was even dry on the pregnancy test, I began hearing the whispers of doubt. *Being a mother is a great big thing—and you're not great enough or big enough.* I was keenly aware that at twenty-six years old, I still needed my mother, and I still needed mothering from others. How could I ever become big enough, strong enough, or wise enough for a wondrous human being to grow within me?

I had heard stories—stories of women who couldn't handle the responsibility and incessant neediness of their children, stories of women who suffered from chemical imbalances and struggled to bond with their children. I heard stories of children with needs that could never be met, of marriages that fell apart, and of women who felt as though they were coming to the end of themselves but not the end of what others needed of them. I feared there would never be enough of me for the task at hand. After the steep, downward rush of a healthy pregnancy that ended in a preterm birth, the fear stayed and grew larger—until the grinding motor of the hospital breast pump began and my body responded. As I had waited for my son's birth, many care providers warned that it may take time for my milk to come in—or that I would never produce enough for him— and that I shouldn't blame myself. I heard them, but their words didn't stop me from worrying.

That first evening, a nurse came to collect my yield and noted with an arched brow, "Wow! Well this should be enough." It didn't look like much, measured in millimeters and minutes on the pump. But on the heels of my fear and doubt, it felt like my first success. It was a sign to me that I may be able to climb out of the hole in which I found myself. It was a sign that I might just be enough after all.

———

At seven months, my child wanted nothing more than to consume me. I was gummed every waking minute: my elbows, eye sockets, cheeks, chin, hip, knee—any surface of prominence was fair game for drool, for gnawing, for running his face and tongue over. If he'd had teeth, I would have been caught between them. At that moment in his life, it was all I could do to resist being devoured and depleted. Any social interaction I had included him, was about him, or was for him. People reached out for him, smiled at him, laughed at him, and, if they spoke to me at all, I responded as him. Dozens of exchanges per day went like this:

"How old are you, precious?"

"Seven months."

"Oh my, are you working on some teeth?"

"Not yet."

"Aren't you just the happiest thing?"

"Always the happiest, except when I'm not."

My son lunged for me on sight, startling whoever happened to be holding him at the time. He wanted to cruise through my day with me, securely attached to my hip. Even a few inches of space between us seemed intolerable for him. And I faded into him, becoming his voice, his nourishment, his vehicle, his resting place, his teething ring, his comfort, his security—his everything. In the face of so much need, surrender seemed the easiest option, even with the knowledge that it was an unsustainable choice. But it is the choice we expect of mothers, whether explicitly expressed or not. We see the expectation in the comments section of any mommy blogger who dares to write about the taxing nature of motherhood: "Why did you have kids if you wanted to sleep?" We hear the expectation in the grocery store, moments after our child is screaming: "Treasure every moment, even this one. One day you'll miss him crying for you." We must enjoy motherhood, treasure it, give ourselves up to it, try harder when we feel depleted, let go of who we were before, nothing matters more than our role as mother. And that's the message that I heard—that I didn't matter, that motherhood mattered more than my selfhood.

The words of institution—"This is my body, broken for you"—used to sound like resignation: "This is all I have, and it is shattered to make room for you." But we are asked to remember this sacrifice at every meal, with every bite of sustaining food we eat with our loved ones. In that remembering, we approach the words from a different angle. Jesus' body has been and will be enough, and the offering of a humble human body can change the course of history, exemplifying God's love and grace for infinity.

Like the call of Christ, the call of motherhood is too often interpreted as only a call to martyrdom—the call for never-ending sacrifice, for sanguine depictions of excruciating pain and suffering, for perfect and docile piety. But this interpretation is weak and all too often damaging. Christ as (only) martyr leaves his followers in a place of discomfort, focused solely on anguish, shame, and woundedness. Likewise, motherhood as martyrdom leaves us in the same place, focused solely on self-denial, physical endurance, and sanctimony. We only need lurk for a few weeks on any number of mother-focused Internet forums or support groups to see motherhood as martyrdom at play. Any topic remotely related to early parenting decisions will have its vehemently vocal proponents and opponents:

> Circumcise. Leave intact.
> Breastfeed. Formula. Exclusive. Both.
> Baby-wearing. Stroller-pushing.
> Cloth diapers. Disposable diapers.
> Baby-led weaning. Purees.
> Organic. Non-GMO. Vegan. Whole.
> Ferber. No-cry sleep training. Co-sleeping.
>   Bed-sharing.
> Working mom. Stay-at-home mom.
> Single income. Dual income.
> Apply for assistance. Tough it out.
> Secondhand. Buy new.

Mothers hear those who oppose them approaching, and they become fearful, no matter how sound their confidence in their decisions. And we shouldn't be surprised after reading this quote from *Godey's Lady's Book* from 1867: "About every true mother there is the sanctity of martyrdom—and when she is no more in the body, her children see her with the ring of light around her head."[11] The emphasis on mother as martyr is not a new phenomenon. The cult of domesticity has not left us. Our great-grandmothers were chided to follow the pattern, and they passed the example down to their children and their children's children. Like the old joke about continuing to cut the ends off a roast because "That's how Mom always did it," we eventually learn that Mom only did so because her pan wasn't big enough for the whole roast. As we strive for martyrdom, we are merely echoing our foremothers who had to shrink to fit a pan that wasn't big enough for them either. But there is a bigger pan and a bigger call.

The words of institution point to the corpus—the body, the Incarnation, the God-with-ness of Jesus. Hearing the call of Christ as a call to the corpus removes the martyr focus. A call to corpus—to being with—is a call to presence and attention but also to celebration. It is a call to eating, drinking, washing feet, and rising again. A motherhood of corpus, then, provides a more sustainable and attractive model. Instead of defining Christlike mothering as an act that leaves us open and bleeding for our children, which mother as martyr does, we can define it as a mother who continues to live her life fully after her children are born. A motherhood of corpus is centered in a divinely created body that continues to be enough. It remembers the full life and created being of the mother. Rather than elevate the children and diminish the mother, a motherhood of corpus expects a whole, integrated family unit on the same level. Suddenly "godly motherhood" doesn't sound so cringe-worthy.

Rather than a constant call to die, what if being shaped like Jesus means answering a ceaseless call to live a life of remembrance? What if, as an echo of that call, we expect to experience abiding joy and radical self-acceptance in motherhood as opposed to only self-sacrifice? What if when we attend to all the implications of Jesus offering his whole life for us, we hear more than a body breaking? What if we listen for more than just the thuds of nails breaking through flesh and lumber, more than the cracks of the whip and the weeping women? What if we look for the Redeemer in the martyr and listen for the laughter that echoes off the empty tomb's walls? When we listen to the words of institution through the frame of life and birth, rather than only death and crucifixion, we hear the proclamation, "This is my body" in a new fullness of meaning.

This is my body, no more and no less. This is what I am made of—my skin, guts, and bones. This is what bears children; this is what breaks for them. The visceral tissue gives way in order for new life to appear. This is the body I have been given, and I offer it without apology or reservation. It is sufficient. These are radical statements to stake our claim on as Christians, as women, and as people trying to figure out how to nurture another beloved child of God.

———

I can be an infinite resource when I'm called to be, when I allow myself to own my body and to trust the divine example who shows me that it is miraculously, mercifully enough, thanks to the grace of God at work in the world.

One day, when I'd fully succumbed to being consumed as often happens in early motherhood, I wrote the following letter to my son:

If I let you consume all of me, neither of us can exist. But if I can breathe, you can grow taller and broader and brighter. I don't know how to explain this to you while you are young. Right now, your concept of self is not separate from me, and I will rejoice and mourn your distance in the future. But right now, for my health, I must police the space between us lest it fade away and you swallow me whole.

Now, if I rewrote the letter, it would be different. Perhaps it would say this:

If I am courageous and willing, I can allow my whole self to be in every bite of me you can take. And somehow, like the miracle of Communion, where every bite is the body and blood of Christ over and over and over again, neither of us will ever run out, and both of us will stay full.

CHAPTER 6

Sharing

*Jesus took a loaf of bread, and after blessing
it he broke it, gave it to the disciples . . .*

—Matthew 26:26

A sun-faded billboard stood on a church's property, which bordered the highway I took to school every day. On it, a light-skinned woman with brown hair stood in front of a gray-blue background with eyes downcast, arms crossed at the wrists over her lower abdomen. Her hair fell over her shoulder, partially obscuring her face. Written next to her in a white italic font were the words "Pregnant and scared? You're not alone." I drove by this sign—and many like it—every day as a child and young woman. After seventeen years of passing the sign,

I surprised myself by hollering at my steering wheel, "Of course she's not alone. She's pregnant! That's literally the reason she's scared because she's *never alone* anymore!"

Shortly after learning I was pregnant, my husband and I started making the time-tested "for two" jokes. Eating for two, drinking for two—in my case, sleeping for two. But that phrase rang in my ears long after the joke concluded: for two, for two, for two. I was never alone. I was two people: a woman and a fetus, a developing body that contained another developing body. I wasn't just me anymore. Somehow, even when by myself, I was a "we." And though at times that felt comforting—like when I was nervous about my child's well-being and then received a volley of kicks to let me know he was okay—so much togetherness was a first for me. I took refuge in the experiences of other pregnant women who talked openly about the strangeness of sharing their body with another autonomous being. Whether through witty articles, books, or online forums dedicated to the experience of pregnancy, I found a community of women who had the same feelings and questions that I did—in all caps, no less: *THERE IS ANOTHER PERSON INSIDE MY BODY, AND IT KEEPS ME UP AT NIGHT, DICTATES MY ACTIONS AND EMOTIONS, AND LITERALLY SCRABBLES AT MY INTERNAL ORGANS. AND EVERYONE IS JUST OKAY WITH THIS?*

Pregnant women often bury or dismiss their questions, honest descriptions, or outright complaints about the strangeness of pregnancy. Discussions of pregnancy are rightly understood as sensitive for both the speaker and her listeners. Whether they are chronically oversold or chronically under-hyped, stories of pregnancy and early mothering—and especially the raw realities that come with sharing our personhood with someone else—are usually met with a mixture of polite indifference or discomfort.

I get it—*placenta* isn't exactly a word everyone uses in mixed company. But our stories of discomfort and dysphoria boil down to one thing: We struggle to reconcile our autonomy as living, breathing women who can do things on our own with the reality that we may require help when standing up from a couch or tying our shoes. By its very nature, an experience of pregnancy demands that we share everything we are and everything we have with a new, growing body—for good and for ill. And for so many of us, that experience runs counter to our hard-fought experience of having rights to our bodies, of learning that we can say no and have that no respected. If we've had to fight hard to claim our autonomy, sharing ourselves with a small stranger—however wanted, loved, and anticipated—can be difficult.

———

Pregnant or not, female-bodied or not, autonomy is not something achieved easily—those who care for toddlers can attest to this truth. Autonomy is something we strive for, throw tantrums for, scream and cry and work toward in fits and starts. Earning our autonomy comes with a lot of mess. It comes with fists balled up and stuck together with strawberry jam, shoes on the wrong feet, arms and head stuck through one hole in a shirt instead of three. Learning our autonomy as humans, the way that we can care for ourselves and live as beings with separate wills from those around us, is difficult work for everyone involved.

Achieving autonomy as a woman is hard fought and hard to give up. Being able to state my identity, my wants, and my needs and not worrying if other people think I'm crazy, overemotional, attention-seeking, or exaggerating is a lofty goal worth attaining. Even with a big personality, a voice that's too loud, and a laugh that echoes around rooms, I still had to work to be seen and heard. By the time I became pregnant, I had finally begun what I thought was the work of feeling comfortable in my own skin. Giving up my autonomy—my control over myself and my sense of being healthily separate from others—was not an easy task. Being in the position of sharing my whole body and, later, my breasts, with someone else whom I did not yet have a relationship with was difficult. After all, the child who I carried, the child from who I could not rest or escape, was a stranger to me. And while I rejoiced in that child's life and gradual emergence, I also found myself desperately wanting a break from pregnancy—some way, other than birth, to hand off the responsibility to someone else and ask, "Can you be the womb for a while? I haven't slept in days, and I'd really like a drink."

Because of my newfound duality—being myself and being on loan to another person—I opened myself to a whole cadre of strangers tasked to care for the two of us. From the confirmation-of-pregnancy appointment all the way through hospitalization and subsequent home visits, my body and my life were opened to stranger after stranger—midwives, nurses, social workers, orderlies, OBGYNs, and maternal-fetal specialists. Before I even knew for certain that there was a life inside me, I had to submit to a transvaginal ultrasound, a procedure that is definitely more invasive than the average ultrasound. What we quickly learn, whether we carry a child in our body or welcome a child into our home as foster parents, adoptive parents, or godparents, is that we must first open ourselves to scrutiny. Strangers will evaluate our health, wholeness, and environment, telling us, in their opinions, what is right and what is wrong. Suddenly, we have goals imposed on us and a new set of rules to follow.

We welcome some of these people—those who are paid to know more than we do and to keep us safe. But there are other voices as well, coming from those who make generalizations based on their individual expertise in their own bodies and with their own children. We are policed, and we are expected to enjoy that policing and respond politely because strangers, however invasive, "mean well." The barista at a coffee shop, for example, questioning whether I need a cup of coffee: "Did you mean decaf?" In order to cope, we tend to stay tight-lipped. We smile politely when people question our food choices, and we say nothing when others make assumptions about our family—or our child— that may be far from the truth. We share our body with another, but we close off some parts of ourselves and share less of our innermost souls.

Our Christian practices assure us that grace is multiplied through sharing. God's acts through scripture repeatedly reinforce this idea. God asks the Israelites in the desert to trust that enough food would appear each day for them so that they wouldn't store up for themselves. Jesus' miracles of feeding at least five thousand people begins with someone willing to share his or her food with others. And the Christian symbol of Communion—modeled by Jesus, who shares a meal with his disciples—exhibits the grace we receive through sharing. At the heart of our faith lies a ritual that cannot be completed alone. Like pregnancy, Communion requires more than one person to participate. As God is in community with Godself—Creator, Incarnate, and Holy Spirit—we are created to be in community with one another.

To demonstrate the way God's family works and to show what the world looks like in God's economy, Jesus inserts a shared meal into the deepest structure of our faith. And then, just in case we missed it, Jesus reiterates his point: As often as you eat and drink, do this in remembrance of me. To remember Jesus, we feed our bodies and one another. To remember Jesus, we forgive one another. To forgive one another, we must know one another. To know one another, we must share with one another. We can share with one another at the Common Table—where we eat and remember together.

Our forebears of faith—from members of the early church to desert fathers and mothers to Christians of the fourteenth century—struggled mightily to describe the holy mysteries that took place around the Common Table. The early church coined its own phrase, *paschal mystery*, in an effort to describe what goes on between God and our fellow celebrants when we take Communion. *Paschal* is derived from Greek (*pascha*) and Hebrew (*pesah* or *pesach*) words, meaning "passing over" or "to be spared" from a sacrifice.[12] As Christians, we may forget that Jesus was crucified during his celebration and observation of Passover, a celebration of the Israelites' deliverance from captivity in Egypt after God's tenth plague against the Egyptians—the death of all firstborn sons. When the angel of death came for the Egyptians, the Israelites were "passed over" by virtue of a sign of lamb's blood on their doorposts. Early Christians—as early as 170 CE—employed the phrase *paschal mystery* to describe and understand Jesus' work as a continuation of God's actions in the Hebrew scriptures.

Our faithful foremothers and fathers of the church understood that what happened on the night when Jesus sat at the table with his friends, what happened on the cross when he was executed, what happened at the tomb when he was resurrected, and what happens when we follow Jesus' instructions and take Communion are beyond total comprehension. We don't understand completely what God is doing when we gather around the Communion table to eat Christ's body and drink Christ's blood and remember what God does in the world, but we can accept these acts as an invitation, a window into God's world. Even though we can't see the whole picture through that window, our coming together around the table gives us a glimpse of what we're supposed to value and how we're supposed to care for God and one another. Even with the help of this phrase, though, Christians still sought images to help them understand what God is doing when they gather together for Jesus' holy feast. For many centuries, the images they turned to revolved around women and mothers.

As early as the second century, Clement of Alexandria used images of pregnant women and nursing women to explain how we relate to Jesus during Eucharist. Additionally, Origen, Irenaeus, John Chrysostom, Ambrose, and Augustine all used language that describes Christ as a mother who carries her children within her own body, generates them from her own matter, sacrifices herself to give them life, nurtures them with her own body, and loves them without fail. These early- and medieval-church thinkers and leaders believed that, unlike other popular deities of the time, the Christian God was best considered in terms of both father and mother. In her work on the subject, Dr. Caroline Walker Bynum writes that these teachers believed that "a God who is a mother and womb as well as a father and animator could be a more sweeping and convincing image of creation than a Father God alone."[13]

The early and medieval church was happy to employ a hefty dose of gender-fluid language and images in their expressions of faith. Our scriptures also provide a glimpse of this, though scriptures employing maternal imagery have been ignored by biblical scholars.[14] Paul feeds his congregants milk instead of solid food (see 1 Corinthians 3:2), describes himself as "a nurse tenderly caring for her own children" (1 Thess. 2:7), and as "in the pain of childbirth until Christ is formed in you" (Gal. 4:19). In addition, many monastics wrote of nursing from Christ's breasts, viewed themselves as carried within his womb or within his wounds from crucifixion, and regularly exhorted their abbots and other leaders to model their behavior as leaders on the examples of women, midwives, and mothers.[15]

As a modern (or postmodern) woman of faith, I was surprised to learn that God and Christ were worshiped and venerated with woman-centric images, language, and concepts, even though I attend a mainline Protestant church that uses gender-neutral language for God. Many Christians agree that God is beyond gender but will hem and haw if someone substitutes *she* and *her* pronouns for *he* and *his*. They will tolerate talk of God-as-mother or celebrate God's womanly attributes on special occasions, such as Mother's Day, but will use male or neuter language only every other Sunday of the year.

Moreover, though the body of Christ has a long history of venerating women, our bodies, and our ways of relating to the world, most Protestant churches didn't begin ordaining women until the twentieth century. Today, only 11 percent of regular church attendees report that their congregation is headed by a woman—a number that's remained stagnant since 1998.[16] More than merely a women's issue, keeping women sidelined and isolated from church leadership and religious language and imagery has concrete personal and systemic consequences. By ignoring the great expanse of women's contributions to Christianity, we've created a system that is self-reinforcing. When the only acceptable pronouns for referring to God are he/him/his, we reinforce the idea that men are more suited to leading and shepherding God's people. When our church historians neglect to teach the stories of female apostles and leaders of the early church—Mary, Mary Magdalene, Mary of Bethany, Eugenia, Lydia, and Junia—those who oppose female leadership in the church can appeal to history and tradition as additional justification for sidelining women's witness. For women of deep faith—especially women who experience God's call to leadership within the body of Christ—the weight of this history matters. Unlike their male counterparts, women have few role models, both biblical and contemporary, to look to as proof that their call is legitimate. They cannot recognize themselves in the life and ministry of the church universal. And if the church universal does not look like the created and beloved children of God, then the body of Christ is missing many of its limbs.

We miss out on a deeper understanding of how God cares for us when we dismiss the many examples of feminine language and imagery present in scripture.

We deny healing to those who need to experience God as Mother as much as they need God as Father. God as Mother language provides imagery of God as nurturer, carrier, and protector to those in need of reassurance, especially those who have suffered abuse at the hands of a man or the absence of a loving male figure in their lives. Because God is in and beyond all gender, expression, and identity, we can use all gender, expression, and identity to read ourselves into God's great story, the body of Christ, and all redeemed creation.

When we fail to recognize the feminine God, we make it difficult to realize God in the feminine. We miss out on pathways, connections, and ways of knowing God, ourselves, and those we love. We miss out on the intimate ways that God fulfills God's name and promise—*God with us*. God revealed in us. Not just some. Not some better than others. Or some more qualified than others.

When we share—our bodies, our lives, our stories, our identities, our pronouns—we expand our understanding and expectations of God. We see more of who God is, who we are, and what we are all called to be. When God herself is seen in all her children, when God herself is glorified in the contributions of all her disciples, when her strength is shown and her mercy renowned, when we experience her as she wishes to reveal herself—only then can we receive her as she offers herself to us.

CHAPTER 7

Acceptance

On the night in which he gave himself up for us . . .
—The United Methodist Book of Worship,
Service of Word and Table I

There is no shame in admitting that, no matter how we come by it, we didn't ask for a lot of what accompanies pregnancy and motherhood. My friend Sadiyeh would never have chosen a journey that included endometriosis, surgeries, and in vitro fertilization (IVF). Julie wouldn't have picked a path marked with losses, HELLP (Hemolysis, ELevated liver enzymes, Low Platelets) syndrome, and gestational diabetes. Raquel would do everything in her power to avoid losing her firstborn daughter to a cord accident at thirty-nine weeks and enduring a stillbirth. Nadia, though thrilled to pieces with her adopted daughters, still grieves for their loss of their first families. Bren didn't want to live with a mental illness that made her choose between her own health by going off her medication long enough to carry a pregnancy and risking her unborn child's health. My own mother, I think, would hesitate if asked about her own losses that preceded my brother's adoption, my birth, and my sister's birth.

All of us who become parents—whether we seek parenthood or find it unexpectedly a part of our lives—come to a point where we must surrender to what's occurred and accept whatever is to come. Whether labor or surgery, court dates or custody battles, needles or general upheaval of our lives, we come to a place of reckoning: If I am to parent a child—this child—then this is what I must do, even if it isn't something I want. This persists in minor trials as well. We parent the children in front of us in the ways that work best for them—even if they are not the ways that work best for us. I was a child who would don sackcloth and ashes if my parents looked sideways at me. My son, on the other hand, is oblivious until I take a very stern tone with him.

The road of motherhood is a road of radical acceptance—of our bodies' capabilities and limitations, of our own scars and strengths. Fertility journeys, pregnancy, adoption, and parenting force us to view ourselves up close with a mirror we've not encountered before. We are faced with everything that we would not have chosen, and, somehow, we are given the opportunity to choose it anyway. Life is not a buffet; instead, we receive what we are served.

We are welcome to transform, discard, ignore, or share what we are given, but this fact remains: We cannot choose what will happen to us.

We cannot know, for example, if Mary would have chosen to be God's Virgin Mother if it appeared as but one option among all infinite possibilities in her life. But we know she did choose it once that option was set before her. Mary, far from the passive vessel that she is often portrayed as, actively accepted what was to come when the angel first visited, when she sang the Magnificat, and when she visited her cousin Elizabeth. I doubt she dreamed of becoming pregnant before enjoying a relationship, before sex. We can reasonably doubt she wouldn't have looked forward to moving through her life pregnant and unwed, armed only with a story even the most faithful among her community would never believe. But she accepted it.

Jesus, we often forget, wanted to avoid the path ahead of him. Though we repeatedly hear in the Gospels that he "set his face for Jerusalem," we encounter him in the garden of Gethsemane, sweating blood and praying all night: "Father, if you are willing, remove this cup from me" (Luke 22:42). In this prayer, I hear my own heart—for myself, for others, and for my child: *God, there must be another way—a better way. I don't want what I know is coming.*

These are the prayers we pray over the toilet as we worry or bleed because of a missed month or a miscarriage. They are the prayers we pray when two lines appear on the test when we had desperately hoped for only one. These are the prayers we pray when our bodies signal that something is not right. They are the prayers we pray when the scans show something wrong with the beloved stranger in our belly. They are the prayers we pray when everything goes right, but we still experience pain in the process—blinding pain, this-is-what-it-feels-like-to-die pain.

I don't know why this is the way things go. I don't know why the wounds have to go before the wins. I don't know why humanity can only continue through women's bodies carrying, bending, breaking, and bleeding. And I don't know why, after that breaking and bleeding takes place, we have to put our hearts on the line over and over in order to raise our children and the ones we love. But Jesus even wondered about the direction his life was going, and that's strangely comforting to me. Even now, we haven't found a way around the trauma of building a family. Even now, we show our love for humanity through suffering, breaking, and death. If Jesus is allowed to wonder at the absurdity of the way things work, surely God wouldn't begrudge us the same. After all—God's been there.

So many of our questions are without true answer. Even as we hold our unanswered questions, even as we wade through all the things we don't want and never chose and decide to choose anyway, we find another side—not an answer but more life to live on the other side of the question. We can accept who we are and what's to come. We can give ourselves up, even if we don't know why it has to be this way. For many of us, this radical acceptance is the most difficult and dangerous part of motherhood. We worry about how our bodies will look and change. We worry about losing ourselves in the work of motherhood, putting our identities and relationships on the backburner in the process. We worry about becoming like the parent from whom we want to distance ourselves. We fear losing our independence and our sense of self. We fear becoming what we have most disdained while looking at other mothers. We fear loving someone so much and over whom we have so little control. We fear we won't love enough.

At some point, we must accept that we are not enough and will never be enough. Not on our own. No amount of our love or mothering will guarantee that our children will feel whole and safe and cared for. If that were possible, mothers in Syria could've stopped the bombs in their tracks, using nothing but the love of their children. Our love and mothering cannot overpower systems of injustice and harm all of their own accord. My mother-love doesn't bring clean water into my kitchen or disinfect the instruments at the hospital. Only our shared life, work, and responsibility can do that. Accepting our bodies—what they need, what they will and won't do—allows us to accept later stages of life when our bodies change. And it allows us to accept our children in their bodies as well.

Far from a passive submission to our circumstance, acceptance is an active move. It's what we mean when we talk about "owning" our successes, our failures, our feelings, and our circumstances. Acceptance sees what's coming next and anticipates the outcome. Unlike getting surprised by something unpleasant or denying what's to come, acceptance focuses on the process we have to move through in order to get the outcome we want. Even as we set our faces for Jerusalem and look down the path toward motherhood—whether we expect to suffer labor, infertility, or loss of privacy and our independence—we anticipate the joyful moments that come in the midst of the worry, pain, and fear. These moments form what my friend Ryan calls a "holy yes," a place where we say yes to something even though we know it's bigger than us and then allow God to fill in the spaces.

———

My own lesson in acceptance came during my hospitalization leading up to my son's birth. Following my frantic trip to the hospital, I was admitted to Labor and Delivery and given drugs to halt what doctors confirmed as premature labor. My doctors couldn't determine what had caused the labor, but they asked to keep me in the hospital for observation over the weekend just in case. During that observation period, my blood pressure began to act up—one reading would measure it at sky-high levels while another would measure a normal 110/70. Finally, I heard the word I'd been dreading: *preeclampsia*, a systemic condition that impacts both mother and child through dangerously high blood pressure, reduced function of the placenta, and numerous other dangers to internal organs, including the liver. To confirm this diagnosis, I collected my urine for a twenty-four-hour period, and the sample was then checked for proteins. If the doctors detected protein in addition to my high blood pressure, they would know that I had preeclampsia.

Besides providing shocking proof of how much urine a pregnant person can produce in a day, my urinalysis was positive for proteins. At thirty-two weeks' gestation, I was admitted to the hospital for a long-term stay. The hospital wouldn't allow me to go home until I had a baby, and I understood that to mean my stay could last hours or several weeks, the latter of which is ideal for a baby's growth but nightmarish for me. I was confined to bed rest, meaning I was only allowed to stand long enough to take myself to the bathroom. Showers had to be taken while seated, and I was allowed one thirty-minute wheelchair excursion per day. All other hours had to be spent in bed. With nothing to do but wait, worry, and endure a bevy of tests, my heart screamed no to all of it. *No, this can't be happening. No, I cannot give birth to this baby yet. No, I can't stand this worry and fear.*

The moment of "holy yes" came when my husband and I were granted a tour of the NICU. In a sort of bitter preview to all the school orientations, apartment tours, or campus admissions that might come to pass in my son's future, my husband and I were granted a guided tour through our hospital's NICU in anticipation of his birth. Because our son was most likely to be born premature and potentially unable to breathe, eat, or regulate his other bodily systems on his own, we knew he was likely to spend a substantial amount of time in the NICU. The idea, of course, was to help give us comfort by introducing us to the caring staff who would look after our son once he made his way into the world. And I wanted the information. I wanted every ounce. My husband wheeled me into the NICU armed with a pen and notebook. They felt to me like my armor and lance. We were in an adversarial position, fighting time and health themselves. And information was my weapon. If I was going to win, knowledge was the way to do it. I took comprehensive notes. I wanted to know everything. I wrote down names, I wrote down what kind of information was written on the whiteboards in every room. I wrote down the jargon I'd want to look up when reunited with my laptop. I wanted to be able to take refuge in knowing what would come next.

Instead, when faced with the sight of too-small babies hooked up to too-big machines, my facade of strength crumbled. No amount of knowledge could protect me from the raw difficulty that we were hurtling toward. Rather than minimizing my fear, the NICU tour revealed it and demonstrated its inevitability. Any illusion of a "normal" birth was destroyed. Our story would include pain, needles, heel sticks, and time apart—nothing I would ever choose for myself, nothing I would ever choose for my child. But it was something I had to accept, something that if I found the ability to say a "holy yes" to, I might find the other side.

Our "holy yes" moments allow us to do two hard, brave things: (1) They allow us to face and name the biggest, scariest, most harmful fears we've ever faced and describe them to ourselves and our support systems. (2) They allow us to tell the truth about what has happened, is happening, or will happen to us. When we face and name the worst thing that happened, is happening, or will happen to us and tell the truth about it—the weird, nuanced, no-holds-barred truth—something strange happens. Friends and strangers surrounding us reach out and hold us up. They show up through comforting text messages and phone calls, through casseroles and cards, through shoulders to cry on and listening ears. Our radical honesty also helps those around us learn that they can be truth-tellers too. They can name their reality and survive to find there is something on the other side.

In a now legendary stand-up routine, comedian Tig Notaro took the stage and opened her set by telling her audience, "Good evening! Hello! I have cancer." She had just learned about her diagnosis, just learned that the disease that took her mother was threatening to take her too. Her fans, familiar with her body of work and her family history, broke into unvarnished reactions. People in the front row openly sobbed. She stood on the stage, microphone in hand, and comforted them, repeating, "Guys, relax, okay? It's fine. I have cancer." Over the course of the set, Tig and her audience moved through a tangible current of grief, anger, fear, and gallows humor. But by the end of the set, the laughter was unbridled. Other comedians remarked that the set was unlike any they'd ever seen, a lesson in what's possible when we share our humanity and vulnerability.

Accepting ourselves, applying our "holy yes" to our circumstances—our bodies, our histories, our failings as parents and as children—allows us to minister to others. Not around our wounds but through them. When we set aside our pretenses, when we allow ourselves to name the path ahead, we begin to move away from fear and into the upside-down power dynamic of God's kingdom: Where we are weakest, we are strongest. Where we are broken, we are blessed. Where we are empty, we are filled. When we come to our end, we make room for a beginning.

CHAPTER 8

Remembering & Storytelling

"Do this, as often as you drink it, in remembrance of me."
—1 Corinthians 11:25

At six months of pregnancy, my belly became an obstacle between me and the steering wheel of my car. Around the same time, I developed a ritual of singing in the car on my morning commute. A strange combination of Cat Stevens, old hymns, Jim Croce ballads, and show tunes accompanied me down the highway. But one song began to stand out, a tune called "Not a Lullaby" from folk duo The Weepies. That song suddenly seemed to be written for us—the self-contained us held in place by my seatbelt. I sang it to my baby every day in anticipation of his arrival, hoping that the studies I'd heard would be true—he might remember it after he was born.

A month later, sleepless and alone in an antepartum unit, Christmas lights winked outside my narrow window. My long-suffering husband had gone home at my urging and demand. "This baby could show up any day, and then who knows what will happen," I said. "Go home and sleep in a real bed while you can." My belly itched where dried flakes of ultrasound gel remained caked on from the bevy of tests earlier in the day. Left sick and alone in the dark, I quietly sang The Weepies tune for us. If we had to stay in an unfamiliar place like this, I hoped I could at least sing us into a semblance of familiarity.

A week later, I stood in front of my son's Isolette. The whiteboard to the side read Ezra Lee, 1970 grams. (That's 4 pounds, 5 ounces.) He sported a nasal cannula to keep his oxygen levels up and an IV for drugs and nutritional fluids and fats. Wires for four different monitors were attached to his body, along with a blood pressure cuff. He was naked but for a diaper—no clothes allowed. His belly was long and flat, and it moved up and down quickly with his breath. My belly was held together with glue, distended and sore. It felt woefully empty, but somehow, I didn't have room to breathe. My lungs had far more real estate to expand into now that he was on the outside of my body, but the air couldn't reach. In a few minutes, I was going home without him and only a massive, industrial-grade breast pump to take his place—the world's saddest consolation prize.

I choked out the lyrics, trying to reassure him that I *would* be here the moment he needed me. But my body knew that the moment he needed me was all of them— every moment. We were built to be a team, and even though it made perfectly logical sense for me to walk out of that room and leave the hospital, every fiber of my being shouted, *Do not leave your baby. This is wrong.* I had to leave but tried to let something take my place. My voice cracked and broke, strangled and then began again. But eventually the song I'd practiced, the song I hoped he'd recognized, broke through. As I walked out, I prayed it would echo in his ears.

The next day, I came back, and he was still there. My breasts, now engorged with the milk that had come in, made it impossible for me to see my belly without aid of a mirror. I asked when he'd been fed overnight, and I smiled when the times lined up with hours I'd wakened to pump. I kept singing and pumping and barely sleeping. He kept eating and grunting and sleeping enough for both of us. The ending line of the song with its certainty—"I'm gonna hold you in my arms"—became a hopeful promise. While the words of the song had tasted bitter and cruel on the night I was discharged and sent home without my child, its faithfulness remained. There were plenty of clouds. The rain fell as tears every time, right as I got outside the door of the NICU. But its words were certain—I didn't care whether he cried as long as I got to carry him home. Without intending for them to, the words became our story—or, perhaps, gave me an avenue to make sense of our story. It transformed into something larger—a way of remembering what we'd gone through and how far we'd come, a portal back to the time when we were in the same body and learning how we'd be in the world together.

It wasn't a lullaby when I sang it; it was a litany.

———

During the Communion liturgy, I once heard a pastor describe our collective action as remembering and retelling the great story, allowing ourselves to be woven into the fabric of the story along with the brothers and sisters in faith who have gone before and the children in faith who will come long after. Suddenly, Communion made sense to me. Despite going through confirmation and checking off each faith-formation box, I felt like I was missing something when I participated in the Communion liturgy. It became rote. I had long ago memorized the entire liturgy (including the clergy lines) and would tune out during the long portions, listening only for the watchwords that signaled a congregational response was approaching.

Once I understood the Great Thanksgiving as retelling the story, my ears perked up. I listened closely for the first time, in new appreciation for what we were doing. I realized that this holy recitation had shaped me into a person who knew the worn, old story of our faith as though it were written on my bones. With the Great Thanksgiving, I could call back to myself across my whole history—sleeping on the shoulder of a friend and pewmate during Sunday service, receiving Communion in the hospital as I sat beside my dying grandfather, and serving Communion just as my fathers and mothers of the faith had done long before. The words of the story, told again and again, became a cornerstone for my own story and connected me to the massive clouds of witnesses who had come before.

These words of institution are some of the first words around which our core Christian practices were built. They remain one of the few things that our entire Christian family tree holds in common. From Eastern Orthodox traditions to American evangelicalism, the words of institution—*This is my body, broken for you. This is my blood, shed for you*—can be found at the heart of all Communion practices. First relayed in 1 Corinthians 11:23-26, the words are attributed to Jesus in the context of the Last Supper. Jesus' words were put to use by early Christians, forming a centerpiece of the communal practice of worship and Eucharist.

Along with these words, early Christians took great care to describe how the sharing of the common meal would take place. Though many Christians experience Communion in a subdued, orderly manner, the early church appears to have been a place of holy commotion. Paul's letters to churches throughout the Roman Empire often contain thoughts and admonishments about how Christians should conduct themselves in their worship spaces, which would have been private homes or loaned spaces. These times of worship focused on the communal meal and on serving everyone who came. Jesus' words echo the God of Abraham, Isaac, and Jacob, who called us to remember who

God is and what God has done for us: "Do this in remembrance of me" (1 Cor. 11:24). Jesus' words encourage us to seek God beyond our minds; we must use our bodies and act with intention. Every time we eat and drink, we are asked to remember Jesus' body and blood. While the Hebrew scriptures ask after our hands, eyes, hearts, and doorposts, Jesus asks after our tables and who we share them with. Jesus asks us to remember God as we feed and are fed.

Eating a meal together creates a family, whether in cheap apartments as young adults, in mess halls as soldiers during basic training, in cafeterias as students, or in prison cafeterias as inmates. The people with whom we sit and enjoy a meal become our family, and God, our sacred memory keeper, asks us to remember that family every time we sit down. In this way, each meal becomes a memorial feast.

This tradition of memorial feasting, interestingly enough, appears to have come to first-century people as an existing standard of practice within the Greco-Roman world. Religious banquets, like the one at the heart of our Christian practice, reinforced the ideology of those who celebrated the feast. Jesus' words in 1 Corinthians, the words that became our words of institution, follow Greek and Hebrew funerary traditions. And they follow the form and practice of words and roles traditionally filled by women.

Women were the primary actors at funeral banquets in antiquity. Their songs of honor and mourning were believed to weave a bridge between the living and the deceased, connecting their death to the future lives of their family and loved ones. The lamenter—again, typically a woman—acted and was viewed by her audience as a "mediator between realms."[17]

For those who have hung around enough church ladies, this may feel familiar. Across denominational boundaries or faith traditions, women play a unique role in memorial action of their communities. Women will often run the meal train, drop off casseroles, set up a funeral spread, organize a chore share, and otherwise strive to care for congregation and community members in sickness or grief. I have long joked that I am actually an "old church lady" in a young woman's body because after years of hanging around my older sisters in the faith, I've fallen into the habit of keeping ingredients for a casserole on hand at any given time.

As a strange side effect of patriarchy, which demands that "boys don't cry" and men only can deal with their emotions privately, women have taken up the work of public grief and care during turmoil. Funerals, memorials, and care for the sick have fallen under the deft hands of women— hands tasked with the work and logistics of remembrance. From the Marys at the tomb to early Christian women to our modern church women in the basement, staying, witnessing, and remembering has long been the work of women of faith.

When we hear God's call to remember, we find yet another place where the experiences of mothers and women offer rich knowledge and points of connection to draw from. Rather than viewing this simply as a commandment from God on high or the plea of a wanted criminal soon to be torn from his friends, the call to remember likewise can be seen in the old ways of our grandmothers and aunts and older sisters in the faith. We can hear it too in the thrum of our mothering hearts—the call to keep hold on what's most true about ourselves and our children. So when we sit down to eat, whether together or apart, the meal will make a family, and we will know whose we are.

———

The act of remembrance goes back even farther than the Communion table. According to the shared stories of our Christian people, God remembers us and asks us to remember God. For example, God remembers Noah (see Genesis 8:1) and the covenant God made not to flood the earth again (see Genesis 9:15). God even reminds Noah of this promise through a rainbow, stretching across the sky (see Genesis 9:16). Throughout the Hebrew scriptures, we read about how God remembers God's people: Abraham (see Genesis 19:29), Rachel (see Genesis 30:22), and the Israelites (see Exodus 6:5). Our stories are filled with God noting us, remembering us, witnessing us, and vowing to remember God's covenant. And after God has made that covenant, God asks us to remember it as well. As Moses and the Israelites leave Egypt, God calls out to them again and again, asking them to remember what God has done for them: "Remember that you were a slave in the land of Egypt" (Deut. 24:22). (See also Deuteronomy 11:2; 15:15;

16:12; 24:9; 24:18.) God follows this imperative with a command: "Therefore I am commanding you to do this" (Deut. 24:22).

This repeated call for remembrance remains at the heart of faithful expression for our Jewish siblings through a practice of reciting the *Shema*. *Shema*, the Hebrew word meaning "hear," refers to passages from Deuteronomy 6:4-9; 11:13-21 and Numbers 15:37-41. This confession of faith goes as follows:

> "Hear, O Israel: The LORD is our God, the LORD alone. You shall love the LORD your God with all your heart, and with all your soul, and with all your might. Keep these words that I am commanding you today in your heart. Recite them to your children and talk about them when you are at home and when you are away, when you lie down and when you rise. Bind them as a sign on your hand, fix them as an emblem on your forehead, and write them on the doorposts of your house and on your gates." (Deut. 6:4-9)

God calls us to remember who we are, who God is, and what God has done in the world. This call of remembrance isn't one of cerebral knowledge. God asks us to remember in our flesh—our heart, hands, and eyes—in our soul, and in our homes. God tasks us with telling God's stories to our children and remembering God even in the clothes we wear. But even when we turn away and our love fails—as some Communion liturgies remind us—God does not turn against us. Even when we forget to remember, God remembers. God remembers not only our sins but also our stories, and our shared stories reveal God as a sacred keeper of memory. When we forget who we are—God's beloved, chosen, and liberated people—God remembers. God, like a mindful parent, can knit us back together with stories that remind us who we've always been, stories that reveal those parts of ourselves that are central to who we are.

———————

I've learned that so much of mothering is remembering— remembering which breast my son nursed from last, where I kept his shot record, who's picking him up from day care, when we gave him the last dose of ibuprofen, where we keep the nasal aspirator. And, for those of us residing in the great state of Missouri, remembering to send off for my child's birth certificate, which can only be done six weeks after birth, ensuring that I was in the deepest part of sleepless haze from caring for a newborn when the time came for that vital task. I finally remembered to get a copy shortly after my son turned two and a half—and only because his new day care required a notarized copy. So much of motherhood is remembering exactly which forms and how many copies are necessary to enroll in day care, elementary school, high school, trade school, college.

Mothers, especially when it comes to childhood, are expected to be the memory-keepers. Children are often given assignments, either in school or in extracurricular activities, that entail asking their parents about their story. Children want answers to questions like, *What was I like as a baby? What was my first word? When did I learn how to walk?* Sometimes the questions are more expansive, asking about extended families, ethnic heritage, and moves from other countries. Parents—and mothers especially—often feel pressured to mentally catalog this information for entry into a baby book or some other record. Additionally, foster and adoptive parents face the task of passing on a story about an experience they may not have witnessed.

This work of remembering can take a toll and is sometimes beyond our grasp. For those of us who struggle with postpartum depression or postpartum anxiety, much of our memory of our early motherhood can be colored by a haze. Worse yet, many of us feel guilt over that haziness, our first "failure" as memory-keeper. Even without the added difficulties of postpartum disorders, the work of remembering can leave us with little room to remember ourselves—our joys, our hobbies, our life before motherhood. Without a way to remember our former selves, how do we make our way back to who we were after the upheaval of welcoming a new child into the family?

I returned to work a little fewer than eight weeks after Ezra was born—only six weeks after he had come home from the hospital. Like the stereotypical new parent, I was all frayed ends, struggling desperately to keep it together. Since he was premature, my baby had the behavior of a two-week-old even though he had the chronological age of an eight-week-old, meaning round-the-clock feedings would continue for many months. I never felt fully in place. At work, I was exhausted and thinking of home; at home, I was exhausted and dreading work. When I tried to think of the things that had helped me cope through sleepless weeks of graduate school and other periods of high stress, my mind went blank.

Feeling disconnected from my life had impacts on the things I held dear: my ability to communicate, my quality of work, my love for activity, and my intimacy with my partner. How could I desire a connection with another person when I was feeling out of sorts with myself? Slowly, gradually, the fog began to lift. Mostly because my son, my husband, and I all learned to sleep again but also because I began telling myself the story of who I was and what had happened to me. I used stories as a method of remembering—as my forebears in faith had long ago. I put my remembrance into action and let that action bring healing.

The stories we tell—the words and phrases we choose—influence the way we remember events. Studies show that when asked how fast a car was going when it *smashed into* another vehicle, people will estimate the speed significantly higher than when asked how fast the car was going when it *contacted* another vehicle.[18] We enact our remembrance by telling stories, whether with words or art or photos or artifacts. Each time we remember—that is, each time we tell the story—we open ourselves to transformation. Telling our stories to others challenges us to view our stories in a different way.

Eleven months after my son was born, I stood up in a bar full of strangers and told our ridiculous birth story—a story that, in all honesty, began long before my son was conceived. I told the story of the previous eleven months and how I had harbored complex feelings about every bit of having a child. I had felt guilty about how easily my husband and I conceived after being told to anticipate struggle and after watching so many beloved friends face disappointment in their path to becoming parents. I had felt whiplash from being in good health to becoming critically unwell overnight. I had felt guilty for being away from my son for the first twelve hours of his life and then being too drugged to sufficiently remember anything about the next twenty-four hours with him. I, the keeper of sacred memory, had missed his entrance and first days in the world, and I would never get them back. What kind of mother couldn't tell her child about his first few moments on earth? What kind of mother couldn't remember seeing her son's face for the first time or the way his small body felt against hers? My son was brand new, and I already felt that I'd failed him—not just in failure to carry his body to term but a failure to tell his story.

I fixated on my and my son's medical reports from our hospitalization. First, the two weeks of reports detailing sudden, intense bleeding, climbing blood pressure, and decreased fetal movement, which led to my eventual diagnosis of severe preeclampsia. Then, following his birth, the daily NICU reports: his weight, blood oxygen saturation, irregular body temperature, and food intake. I read and reread them three to four times per week in the months following his birth. My response was one common for trauma victims: I searched for answers, for the whys amid the whats. I searched for clues about the future—Would this happen again? Could it? Moreover, I struggled to form the story—his story. All the while, I was oblivious to the fact that I was trying to piece together my own story—a net with which to carry the bits and scraps of memories that felt like a million shattered pieces.

Eventually, I grew strong enough to call my trauma *trauma*. I made friends with it, even though I hated when it would sneak up on me and resurface old, forgotten feelings. I knew I had to let it breathe, so I stood up in a bar and told a story about fear and blood and the agony of telling my husband that, if everything went wrong and he had to make an impossible choice, I still wanted him to pick me. I ended by letting everyone know that we—my son and I—are fine, that the story has a happy ending. I said that one year later, I looked back and found that I had survived. I cried in the telling, and my audience did too. But I walked away lighter. Though I'd been telling myself all along that my son and I were okay, that there was no reason to shame or blame myself for what had happened—I was only able to believe it when I told the story aloud.

My method of public grief and self-disclosure isn't the ticket for everyone. Not everyone will feel healed by baring his or her soul to strangers. But we all have stories that beg to be remembered, stories that, even in their pain, are important to tell. Our vulnerabilities, our insecurities, our

unearned feelings of shame and indebtedness are transformed when we expose them to the light. And in their
place, a new truth emerges—God's story comes forward.
Like an exasperated grandmother reminding us, "You
always were headstrong!" Like a loving mother, hoping
to bring her child comfort, "Even as a child, you were a
fighter. You can get through this." Remembering our stories—remembering God's stories—always brings us back
to the same starting point: "You were there—in Egypt, in
the hospital, on the bathroom floor—and I was with you. I
am your God. I remember you."

CHAPTER 9

Being Made One

By your Spirit make us one with Christ, one with
each other, and one in ministry to all the world.
— The United Methodist Book of Worship,
Service of Word and Table I

We never stop belonging to each other. Our fates are always inextricably tied to others— first by umbilicus, later by heartstrings. Jesus' incarnation, death, and resurrection prove once and for all that nothing—no force, no sin, no shame, no system, no power, no claim—can separate us from God's love and redemption.

Our bodies bear witness to this truth as well. Even after we divide one and end with two, we never stop belonging to each other. With every pregnancy, gestational bodies inherit small communities of cells from their children.[19] At a cellular level, our bodies testify to the truth and existence of the lives we carry and the people who first carried us. Whether our children died before their first breath or our children are separated from us by tragedy or geography, they are imprinted throughout our bodies, and our own genetic makeup is irrevocably written on our own mothers' bodies. The stories written on our bodies are written on our souls as well.

Try as we might to compartmentalize, we cannot escape our lives and experiences. My upper lip will always bear the monument to my birth and repair—no philtrum in sight but a slight scar all my own, the last remaining sign of my cleft lip. Part of my left knee will always belong to the nine-year-old who tripped over the window unit in my friend's bedroom. My first set of stretch marks echo my sixteenth year, when I left tenth grade as a B cup and returned to eleventh grade as a D. Our favorite sports, hobbies, ailments, age, and genetic lineage are written into our bones. Should our skeletons someday cross paths with future specialists, they may be able to tell which shoulder we used to keep the phone against our ear, which hand we favored to anchor our books or iPads as we read into the night. Every pain, every abuse, every joy, and every fault are ours forever. Body and soul. Action and reaction. Choice and consequence.

The side effect of hanging around with God is that we are "made one with Christ, one with each other, and one in ministry to all the world." But we don't always read the fine print. In God's plan, we hitch a ride into God's world to come. The parts of myself that I don't want to reconcile aren't left out of God's radical work. Those parts have to get made one with Christ too. If I were to send Jesus a text message about that bit, it would simply consist of three eye-roll emojis. *Really?* I ask. *I have to bring my high-strung inner critic along too? She's terrible. I try never to bring her anywhere. She's not invited to my eternity.* But we don't get to leave ourselves behind and fade into an indistinct pool of creation energy. Jesus insists on redeeming the whole kit and caboodle. Turns out, being made one with Christ means being made one with ourselves too.

But if our scars come with us—and, after all, they came with Jesus—it stands to reason that our scars are part of the body of Christ. Our breasts and bodies and bellies that were never quite the same, our shoulders that ache from bouncing a baby all night long, every spot we were taught to criticize, every feature we grew to hate—all are caught up in the gospel proclamation: This is my body. This is Christ's body.

We never stop belonging to each other—including ourselves. And this is why it feels radically important to shout loud and clear that women's bodies are not less than males, that there is no hierarchy of body parts or their functional abilities that make some of us better images of God than others. We resemble our Creator, and, therefore, our created selves help us piece together God's stunning likeness.

Our understandings of God are imbalanced at best and warped at worst when they fail to incorporate the unique power, beauty, and diversity of all God's people. We miss out when we exclude others, and we exclude all who we don't intentionally include. We miss out when we overlook, sideline, or dismiss non-male, non-able-bodied, non-cis, non-white people as images and icons of God. If I am to be "one with Christ, one with each other, and one in ministry to all the world," as my United Methodist preachers recite over each the Communion table, I must recognize Jesus in every body before me. I need to proclaim God's image in every body. The body of Christ, the church, and the communion of saints must proclaim God's image in me. All of me. Not in spite of my woman's body but because of it—because of the experiences written on my skin and bones, because of the parts of me that continue to dwell in my mother's body, and because of the parts of my child that continue to live on in me.

We are uniquely equipped to witness to something true, and the church is incomplete without that witness. When we are made one, we don't have to worry about what's deemed fit for the consumption of "polite company." When we are made one, our stories are no longer relegated to a genre or niche of "women's issues." When we are made one, the men in my life can take refuge in the Magnificat as enthusiastically as I revel in the story of Joshua. Surely, the truth sets us free, but a truth that minimizes half the world makes a world only half-free. Full freedom is not freedom from one another but freedom to be fully present with one another in our distinctions and diversity.

The first time I told another woman about hearing Christ's words—"This is my body"—as I washed my breast pump parts and laughed at my wrecked and ravaged body, tears sprang to her eyes. She tried to blink them back, but soon my tears joined hers. "That's really cool," she said. "I don't know why I've never thought of that before." So I mentioned it to another woman and another—churchy friends, atheist friends, and friends from radically different Christian traditions. Ordained women, lay women, child-free women, and women still hoping for the children they desired. Most of the time, my friends and acquaintances grew teary or quiet, but they often repeated the words, "I don't know why I've never thought of that before." Whether these women had spent their lives encircled in the arms of the church or moving through the ether of our Christian-dominant nation, it didn't matter. None of us had been able to link Jesus' words with our own experience. By omission or commission, we were thoroughly taught that "This is my body" was a phrase for select and special use—that its gospel proclamation could never be said about our own.

No matter what we've been told, we're not left out of the story. We've never been left out of the story. Though our experiences have been resigned to a market segment, though we've been burned at the stake for boldly believing that God has called us to greatness, though our bodies have been ignored or understudied, leaving us vulnerable to diseases and ailments common throughout history, though our apostleship has been and continues to be subverted, subdued, or underestimated, Jesus' story is our story—a birth story. Not a story that celebrates the fact that we're all God's children while demonstrating that God plays favorites but a story that moves us in organ-shifting, body-swelling, new-life-emerging ways.

We lay claim to God's glory in the same way God chose to reveal it—in our flesh. Not in spite of it but because of it. To help us practice this, I dream of throwing an enormous party where all present are handed temporary tattoos that say, "This is my body." And while we laugh and sing and eat and drink together, we will take turns pressing wet washcloths to our flesh—the flesh we struggle to love, fail to claim, or try to hide from ourselves and others. We will share our stories of harm and hurt, of reparation and reconciliation, of joy and justice. We will remove the washcloth and peel back the paper, seeing the bold words on our skin for the first time.

This is my body.

This is my body.

This *is* my body.

This is *my* body.

This is my *body.*

Every scar, every cell, every dimple of cellulite, every wrinkle, every joint, every inch, every pound, and every story—this is my body, and it is sufficient. At the end of the party, under the light of stars or streetlights, our bodies will make that gospel proclamation to anyone who witnesses us. What a fierce and wonderful sight to behold. Perhaps it could change the world. When we behold ourselves and one another, embodied, alive, testaments to God's work and love in the world, maybe that's when we find ourselves feasting at God's endless table—there, where God's work is finished; there, where God's work is begun.

DISCUSSION GUIDE

Chapter 1: Incarnation

The Incarnation is one of the great mysteries of our Christian faith: God of all becomes flesh, God-with-us, who submitted "to the point of death—even death on a cross" (Phil. 2:8). In this act, God announces that our embodied selves are important and necessary to God. Yet, for many women, connecting to God in, with, and through their bodies is difficult because their relationship to their own bodies is strained. Just as we have inherited a long tradition of women proclaiming God's word and works—from the women at the tomb to the desert mothers, from medieval mystics to modern preachers—we also have inherited a long tradition of denying our embodied, female selves in order to do that work.

This chapter contends that glorying in the Incarnation and radical vulnerability of God-with-us, especially as we understand that vulnerability through an intimate understanding of pregnancy, birth, and early motherhood, gives us a deeper understanding of God's salvific work and a greater understanding of our own embodiment, vulnerability, and freedom to love and serve God *because of* and *with* our whole female identities rather than in spite of them.

- What messages did you receive about bodies as a child from your family, your church, and your faith? Think back to some of your early memories either in an extended family setting or in a faith community. How did others react to you or talk to you about your body? How did these messages continue to shape your attitude about yourself as you grew into adulthood?

- When have you sensed an attitude shift in your family or church, especially in response to your body and how you should comport yourself? (The author cites puberty as a sudden shift. Other experiences might surround illness, loss of mobility, or other bodily changes.)

- Antoinette Gutzler, MM, proposes that Jesus' ministry on earth, especially to the sick through physical touch, demonstrates that bodies themselves can serve as gospel proclamation.[20] How does hearing that God celebrates your whole, embodied self—because of who you are rather than in spite of it—change your feelings about your body?

Chapter 2: Prayer

This chapter studies the similarities between two communal practices: feeding an infant and prayer. Using each practice as a lens to view the other, we see parallels that help us understand them in a new light. Feeding an infant—or caregiving or meeting another person's needs—can be taxing and leave us sleepless and spent. It also can be holy and beautiful. Likewise, prayer, which we often regard as quiet, holy, and comforting, can become rote, exhausting, or dry.

The author connects the routine of caring for an infant and the act of regular prayer, calling both a "holy interruption" that can reset our orientation to our work and our daily lives. When we are called to stop and feed—or stop and pray—we allow ourselves the space to consider matters beyond work projects, running errands, or other tasks that dominate our thinking. For those few minutes, we connect with something bigger than ourselves—whether the biological need to feed and share closeness with someone in our care or the call to connect with the Creator of the world.

- What prayer practices nourish you? What aspects of prayer frustrate you?
- The author draws a parallel between the work of nursing or feeding a child and the ancient practice of praying the Hours, in which persons observe five to seven scheduled prayer times during the day. In your experience of feeding a child or praying the Hours, what were the holy or difficult moments of those practices?

How did those holy and difficult moments overlap or converge?

- Scripture tells us that God relates to us like a nursing mother: "Zion said, 'The LORD has forsaken me, my Lord has forgotten me.' Can a woman forget her nursing child, or show no compassion for the child of her womb? Even these may forget, yet I will not forget you" (Isa. 49:14-15). Nursing mothers who are unable to nurse or pump experience physical pain if they go too long between feedings. Additionally, they may experience spontaneous letdown, that is, milk flowing freely as a result of their body's preparedness to feed a child. What does this image tell us about God's heart for us? How does understanding prayer as an act of connection and nourishment change the way we pray?

Chapter 3: Breaking, Giving & Sacrificing

This chapter compares Jesus' words at the Last Supper and his actions during the Crucifixion to the work of mothering, parenting, and caregiving. The author reminds us that though we were born through an act of breaking and sacrificing, none of us has a blueprint on how to do that well. Likewise, though our bodies eventually will succumb to death, we are unprepared for dying.

• We hear Jesus' words at the Last Supper and the words of institution during our Communion practice as words about death. But Jesus' words, "This is my body, broken/given for you; This is my blood, shed/poured out for you," also provide an accurate depiction of birth. One body breaks and spills blood so that another life can begin. When we view Jesus' work on the cross and our remembrance of Communion as acts of birth rather than death, what changes? How does this new perspective help us relate to the sacrament differently?

• When the author made a connection between the words of institution and birthing a child, she could identify with Jesus in a way she never had before. Though Jesus had a male body, understanding his sufferings as akin to what women's bodies experience in birth allowed her to see herself and Jesus differently. How have you felt estranged from descriptions or images of God or Jesus? How have you felt connected?

• Just as bodies break and rebuild, so must all families. Through adoption, foster parenting, divorce, and death, families experience breaking, giving, and sacrificing. How has your own family broken or shifted over time? What sacrifices have you or your family members made? What have these sacrifices taught you about God, yourself, and your family unit?

Chapter 4: Blood

The chapter opens with an observation about the role of blood in the Bible and how we often are taught that the first human blood spilled was from one brother murdering another. Instead, the author encourages us to remember that the first significant amount of human blood spilled was from the very first birth: Eve giving birth to Abel.

- If we train ourselves to focus on the first birth as much as we do the first death, how can we reorient what the scriptures tell us about ourselves, God, the world, and creation?

- What did your faith tradition teach you about Mary? How do you relate to her? How is her life important to your personal understanding of faith?

- The author refers to the Incarnation as "God fully vulnerable." What does it mean to worship a God who was subjected to the dangers of pregnancy, delivery, and infancy—including diseases, violence against women, maternal depression, and problems with nursing? What does it mean for us to follow a God who allowed God-self to be radically dependent upon human beings?

Chapter 5: Being Consumed

This chapter focuses on the way early motherhood and parenthood can be all-consuming, leaving us feeling spent and broken, as though we have nothing more to give. Additionally, it examines the cultural forces that expect parents—especially mothers—to adopt the attitude of martyrs who continuously sacrifice themselves and ignore their own needs in order to satisfy their children. Jesus models a radically different perspective, stemming from the idea that the simple eating and drinking and coming together of Communion has sustained God's people for the last two millennia. Therefore, committing to being ourselves—no more, no less—allows us to be enough for our children, our families, and the work God has called us to do.

- Name a time when you struggled with inadequacy or not being "enough" for your loved ones, for your community, or for your church. Where are those feelings rooted?
- When do you feel most like yourself? What joy do you experience in that situation?
- Imagine if someone you love were to say, "You are enough. You possess exactly what you need in order to grow into what God has in store for you." How would you react? If you believed your loved one's statement to be true, what new challenges or opportunities would you take on?

Chapter 6: Sharing

This chapter focuses on the all-encompassing and often difficult ways that pregnancy and motherhood require women to share themselves with their child, their care providers, their partners, and the world at large. Just as women share their bodies with their children, Jesus shared his body with his disciples. Women and Jesus both break open their bodies and shed their blood in order for their beloveds to have new life. In centuries past, the medieval church used "God as mother" language as an access point for understanding the unique ways that God cares for us, God's beloved children.

- When you describe God's characteristics, do you use male-centric language or female-centric language? Why?
- How would your experience of worship or your faith community change if it incorporated female or "God as mother" language and imagery?
- What parts of your identity (if any) are not welcome in church spaces?

Chapter 7: Acceptance

This chapter invites us to consider all the ways we actively accept our difficult experiences and how that acceptance allows us to endure things we'd never expect. In our Christian life and in taking Communion, God calls us to accept our faults and shortcomings, accept what God offers to us, and accept our responsibility as guests of God's ever-expanding table. God welcomes us and our baggage, and God welcomes others too, ever calling us to make more room at the table.

- How has radical acceptance helped you make room in your life for disappointment, heartbreak, and unexpected hardship? Describe a time when you experienced a moment of "holy yes."

- What parts of yourself are you still working to accept? What parts can you claim using Jesus' words: "This is my body, broken. This is my blood, shed"?

- Think of your loved ones, those who you love and those who love you. Recall a time when you accepted or received radical acceptance from a loved one. How did this acceptance change your relationship?

Chapter 8: Remembering & Storytelling

This chapter focuses on remembrance as a key component of what Jesus asks us to do in the work of the Last Supper: Do this "in remembrance of me." God always has called upon God's people to remember—first through God's commandments in Deuteronomy and again throughout scripture. God calls us to remember who God is and who we are and to tell the story of God's work in the world, bearing witness to what God has done for us. This remembrance and storytelling play an important role in how we are shaped. The stories we share around our family tables hold power and tell us who we are and what we value. Similarly, the stories we tell about ourselves and what we have endured can become conduits for healing as we face past trauma.

- If you knew you were going to die but had one last chance to dine with family and friends, how would you ask them to remember your life and legacy after you are gone? What can you learn from Jesus, who asked to be remembered each time you gather with others for a meal?
- When have you taken on the role of memory-keeper for your family or been given that role by someone else? Did you take the responsibility of remembering with joy or with frustration? Why?
- What stories do you tell yourself about who you are and your work in the world? Who helped you craft them? How do these stories reflect the freedom and love of the gospel?

Chapter 9: Being Made One

This chapter begins with the following words: *We never stop belonging to each other.* That saying later grows to, *We never stop belonging to each other—including ourselves.* Jesus' work on earth and on the cross and the work of the church in the world are to make us one with God and all creation. This means we are made one with ourselves too—even those parts of ourselves that we would rather hide, avoid, or deny. In order to be made one with God and each other, we are also made one with ourselves as God created us to be. We are re-membered into the body of Christ with and through our own bodies, scars and all.

- When you imagine an eternity in God's kingdom, which parts of yourself would you rather leave behind than have redeemed? Why?

- When Jesus appears to the women at the tomb and, later, to his disciples, they recognize him by his wounds. Even in his resurrected body, Jesus carries the scars of what he has endured. The author believes that your scars and your body are important to Jesus' work and the body of Christ. How do you react to this idea? How would your service and ministry change if you allowed your scars to guide your work as part of the body of Christ?

- Imagine taking a pen and writing Jesus' words on your body: "This is my body." (Or, if you prefer, take a pen and do this!) What parts of your body most need Jesus' words? What parts of your body do you struggle to claim? What parts of your body most proclaim the gospel?

NOTES

1. Irenaeus, *Against Heresies*, Book V, Chapter VI in *Ante-Nicene Fathers: The Apostolic Fathers, Justin Martyr, Irenaeus*, eds. Alexander Roberts, D.D., and James Donaldson, LL.D., vol. 1. (Peabody, MS: Hendrickson Publishers, Inc., 2004), 532.

2. Catholic doctrine—and therefore much of church history—holds that Mary was "ever Virgin." Her lack of sin was tied to her abstention from sex, even after Jesus was born.

3. Caroline Walker Bynum, *Jesus as Mother: Studies in the Spirituality of the High Middle Ages* (Berkeley, CA: University of California Press, 1982), 132.

4. David Biale, *Blood and Belief: The Circulation of a Symbol Between Jews and Christians* (Berkeley, CA: University of California Press, 2007), 5.

5. Maria Mar Perez-Gil, "Mary and the Carnal Maternal Genealogy: Towards a Mariology of the Body," *Literature & Theology* 25, no. 3 (September 2011): 297–311.

6. Saint Bridget of Sweden, *Birgitta of Sweden: Life and Selected Revelations*, ed. Marguerite Tjader Harris, trans. Albert Ryle Kezel (New York: Paulist Press, 1990), 120.

7. Perez-Gil, "Mary and the Carnal Maternal Genealogy," 300.

8. Ibid., 299.

9. Ibid.

10. Saint Bridget of Sweden, *Birgitta of Sweden*, 203.

11. "A Mother's Love," *Godey's Lady's Book* 74 (January–June 1867): 39.

12. "The Paschal Mystery," *Living in Christ* (Winona, MN: Saint Mary's Press, 2010), 1.

13. Bynum, *Jesus as Mother*, 134.

14. Beverly Roberts Gaventa, *Our Mother Saint Paul* (Louisville, KY: Westminster John Knox Press, 2007). Kindle edition.

15. Bynum, *Jesus as Mother*, 147.

16. Mark Chaves and Alison Eagle, *Religious Congregations in 21st Century America* (Durham, NC: Department of Sociology, Duke University, 2015). http://www.soc.duke.edu/natcong/.

17. Angela Standhartinger, "Words to Remember—Women and the Origins of the 'Words of Institution,'" *Lectio Difficilior*, January 2015, http://www.lectio.unibe.ch/15_1/pdf/standhartinger_words_to_remember.pdf.

18. Elizabeth F. Loftus and John C. Palmer, "Reconstruction of Automobile Destruction: An Example of the Interaction Between Language and Memory," *Journal of Verbal Learning and Verbal Behavior* 13, no. 5 (October 1974): 585–89.

19. Viviane Callier, "Baby's Cells Can Manipulate Mom's Body for Decades," *Smithsonian Magazine*, September 5, 2015, http://www.smithsonianmag.com/science-nature/babys-cells-can-manipulate-moms-body-decades-180956493/.

20. Antoinette Gutzler, MM, "Re-imaging the Body of Christ: Women's Bodies as Gospel Proclamation" in *Body and Sexuality: Theological-Pastoral Perspectives of Women in Asia*, eds. Agnes M. Brazal and Andrea Lizares Si (Manila, Philippines: Ateneo de Manila University Press, 2007), 172–86.